Retreads

Also by Prudence Mackintosh

THUNDERING SNEAKERS

Retreads

Prudence Mackintosh

Doubleday and Company, Inc., Garden City, New York
1985

Many of these chapters have appeared, in slightly different form, in *Texas Monthly*.

Chapter 9 originally appeared as "Aw Mom, Do We Have To?" in *Dallas Life*, June 6, 1982.

Chapter 5 originally appeared in *Ladies' Home Journal*, May 1984.

Library of Congress Cataloging in Publication Data

Mackintosh, Prudence.
  Retreads.

Mostly slightly revised articles originally published in Texas monthly.
  1. Child rearing—United States—Addresses, essays,
lectures.   2. Boys—United States—Addresses, essays,
lectures.   I. Title.
HQ769.M2356   1985   649'.1

ISBN 0-385-18893-5
Library of Congress Catalog Card Number 85-4351

For John, Jack, Drew and William

Contents

Retreads

Preface

IN MY first book, *Thundering Sneakers*, I chronicled seven years of my life as the mother of small boys—Jack, Drew and, finally, William. I needed at least one more arm in those days just to get my brood across a busy intersection. In times of bloody emergencies or during plagues of chicken pox (my husband caught it too), I sometimes desperately looked around for the *real* mother to take charge.

I wonder if I've become the *real* mother. I instinctively answer any child who yells, "Mother," in a public place. I drive a station wagon, and my right arm swings out in a protective reflex when I brake suddenly, even if I have no small passengers. I can clean up any substance except cat vomit without gagging noticeably. I can also receive and dish out guilt with the best of them.

On the other hand, I'm not tough enough for teenagers yet. I handle slammed doors, raised voices and hurt feelings the way I always have. I cry. Trying to console our fourteen-year-old who is impatient to outweigh his mother, I say, "Your Dad and I understand what you're going through. I was less than five feet tall in high school, and I think your father was still growing when we married."

"You knew this, and you *still* had children?" he responds with incredulity.

I've instructed his twelve-year-old brother to marshal his hormones for at least six months. Only one on the irrational seesaw at a time, please.

The magazine editor, childless at the time, who persuaded me to write "something about being a mother" just before my thirtieth birthday, ten years ago, said then, "You don't seem any different from the girl I knew in college, but I want you to write about how your life has changed." As I edited galleys with him by phone, I pacified the baby by allowing him to dump boxes of paper clips all over the floor. The three-year-old could sometimes be persuaded to stop swinging on the telephone cord by an offering of cookies before lunch, but he frequently occupied himself by making traps in my kitchen with twine. I sometimes hung up the receiver to find the baby's high chair, the kitchen cabinets, the refrigerator door handle and my left ankle ensnared in his elaborate web. My life *was* changing, and in odd moments I recorded it as honestly as I could. I believed, as perhaps I still do, that if I could just get these daily absurd moments on paper they might make more sense. They seldom do, but the act of writing about them, becoming the observer instead of the participant, sometimes gives me enough distance to take it all less seriously.

I turned forty this year. John, my attorney husband, who sighs and yells a lot at the dinner table, is forty-two. We began some conversations in the early seventies that we're still trying to finish. Jack, the firstborn, for whom I wore miniskirted maternity dresses, is fourteen. Drew, who seemed to be seven for an inordinate time, is suddenly twelve. Think of him in a hammock with a dog licking his face. William, the delicious blue-eyed baby who rendered us unfit for restaurant booths, is a gap-toothed seven-year-old full of riddles. Their toddler years read like science fiction to me now.

Diaper rash ointment has been replaced with Desenex for athlete's foot. Handprints are higher on the walls. The wear and tear these boys inflict on me is less physical than it once was. The pleasures they bring, more subtle. Oh, I still lose a little sleep rubbing charley horses out of fast-growing legs, and the sneakers (much more expensive now) still thunder overhead and in the drier. But in these middle years, my sons have more than my left leg entangled—and not in kite twine. They have my heart caught in more complicated webs of shared life experience.

Stirrings of adolescence in the eldest tell me it's time to write these middle years down as a sort of protective "resouling" before the sneakers begin in earnest to kick against us and finally to run free.

December 1984

1 She Followed Me Home, Mom, Honest

ROSE CAME to our house on a Sunday afternoon the week before school was out. As Drew said, "I never thought I'd love a girl so much." She is an old-fashioned sort of girl with impeccable manners, intelligent eyes, honey-colored hair, and a cold nose. Rose, as Drew and Jack named her within the hour, is a Shetland sheepdog.

"She just wanted to come home with us," the two boys shrugged when I pressed for details as to how she came to be in our yard. I dutifully reported her to the neighborhood police, then sat on the front porch fully expecting a frantic owner to be circling the block. The scene in my front yard could have been a Norman Rockwell sketch. Despite my sons' fascination with the levers of those quarter-gobbling video games or their longings for digital watches that report the time in all the capitals of the world, they will still play ball with a dog as long as she has breath to retrieve.

No owner called to claim our secondhand Rose that afternoon. Winded from having to perform for every child in the neighborhood, she finally lay down beside me on the front step while I petted her silky coat. The neighborhood kids scattered to scavenge dog food from their own pantries. I had often stroked our old tomcat the same way, but his omniscient stare and contented motor rarely invited conversation the way this dog's expressive eyes did.

"Where are you from, Rose? Where are your babies?" I asked. A glance at her underbelly revealed that she had recently weaned pups. I liked her even more. How had she retained her calm demeanor amid a litter of demanding puppies? Or had she just run away for a little peace and quiet? I assured her that I knew how she felt and that if she hung around here for the next few days there would be plenty of nap time, since the boys were still in school. William, my youngest, sat patiently in my lap during this monologue, then said, with some exasperation, "Mom, she doesn't talk."

Over dinner we discussed her other virtues while she waited loyally on the back steps. John and I, of course, tempered this discussion with assurances that the dog's owner would certainly call within twenty-four hours. She had no collar, but Rose was simply too well trained and too well groomed to remain unclaimed. For that matter, she might go home during the night; we had no backyard fence to restrain her. And, no, we couldn't keep her in the house. Instead, the boys made her a bed on the back porch with beach towels and their own pillows.

Drew and I raced each other downstairs the next morning to see if she had stayed through the night. She greeted us both with all the tail wagging due her real master. At breakfast I couldn't talk either of my school-age sons into printing a sign to post on the school cafeteria bulletin board, so I did it myself: "Found: Beautiful and well-trained female Shetland sheepdog without collar Sunday afternoon near our house. Contact Jack or Drew Mackintosh."

The notice at school brought no response, nor did the animal control officer have any record of missing shelties. Over the next few days Rosie and I took walks without a leash while the boys were at school, at first in search of her master but later just for the fun of it. I already rather liked what she was doing to the pace of our lives. Walking was what I always intended to do but never seemed to find the spare time for. With the dog, I found the time. The boys were establishing their own rituals with her after school. William quizzed Rosie about her puppies a lot, and any time she wandered off our porch he ran inside to announce, "I think she's going off to lay some more babies." Jack concerned himself with the practical matters. Did she have plenty of food and water? Was I sure that I had bought the right kind of food? How many days before we could claim her as our very own? What was I going to do about a fence?

Drew never tired of rolling in the grass with her and letting her lick him from ear to ear. "I just never thought a girl would want to play ball so much and chase me," he said. "Rosie and I have our special chair, and we sit together when we're through playing ball. She never jumps up on the cushion until I invite her." Somehow, I didn't mind that a sweaty boy and a dog had usurped my only throne, the wicker chaise on the side porch.

This dog was too good to be true. Although I was still mentally composing an ad to run in the weekly newspaper and scanning the lost-dog notices, I was as reluctant as the children were to answer the phone. As a friend said, "Getting a dog like that is like having a baby who is toilet-trained, sleeps through the night, and says 'please' and 'thank you' when you bring him home from the hospital." By Thursday, secondhand Rosie had become so much a part of the family that John and I berated ourselves for

having denied our sons this experience for so long. As
Drew said, "Mom, a cat just won't jump up and lick you in
the face."

Dogs had undeniably been an important part of my
childhood. Buttons and Bows were good ole 1950s "I like
Ike" cocker spaniels. They didn't hunt or do anything else
very well except love us. I spent so much time away from
my first-grade classroom returning Bows, the female, to
our yard a block from school that in the second grade Mr.
Edwards, the principal, relented and allowed her to sit
beside my desk. My teacher, Miss Hazel Kennedy, even
gave her a report card and promoted her to third grade.

In retrospect, Buttons and Bows seemed like oafish dogs
who were always cast as the straight men in my older
brother's comedy routines. He carefully trained Bows to
roll over for cookie rewards, but when she performed
publicly he always ate the cookie himself. The two of us
never tired of teasing the dogs at the back screen door:
"You wanna what? You wanna come in?" When we had
them barking and leaping in anticipation my brother
would suddenly throw open the screen door, and the pair
of them would careen across the slick linoleum, unable to
stop before they banged their heads on the legs of the
breakfast table.

Because leash laws were nonexistent then, we knew
every dog on our street as well as we knew the neighbors.
Gruff and cantankerous Teddy, who lived next door at the
Prud'hommes', was always on hand to eat our dogs' food if
they failed to appear promptly at feeding time. My
brother and I discovered that we could get Bows to eat
almost anything by saying, "Better eat it, Teddy's gonna
get it."

Although I'm sure our spaniels were worthless as watch-
dogs, they had a strong sense of their turf. We had only to

mention the name of Patsy, the lean wolfish-looking mongrel who occasionally wandered into our yard, to send the pair into a frenzy. To keep her sanity, my mother insisted that we spell P-a-t-s-y in the dogs' presence.

Buttons was with us only a couple of years. He never overcame his penchant for chasing automobiles, and one morning, only minutes after cold-nosing my brother out of bed, the dog lay strangely silent in the street. My dad's editorial in the newspaper the next day read:

> The dog tragedy came to our house
> yesterday just as it must come inevitably
> to all families who allow dogs to curl up
> around their hearts. . . .
> There were no tears at first. There
> was only misery in the eyes of the boy,
> only the questioning look that asks, "Why
> did it have to happen to him? Why does it
> have to happen to me?" . . .
> It is another paradox of life that
> little dogs must die so little boys can
> learn to grow up. . . .

Bows lived five more years. After she died we never got another dog. Maybe it was because we moved to a busier street near downtown, or maybe it was because by then I was a teenager. My friend Kay still had her dog, and I sometimes noticed him through the window of her bedroom, where we regularly pored over issues of *Seventeen* magazine. Pathetic old Mac, a Scottish terrier, would nose his well-chewed rubber ball to the top step of the back porch, then shove it off and chase it. Such a lonely game.

Regardless of the pleasures Rosie might give our boys and John and me, the facts of dog ownership have changed a great deal in the past thirty years. What once seemed to be every child's birthright now has to be considered a luxury item in the family budget. In our case, of course, the dog would require a fence. Registering the dog and securing its tags would cost twenty dollars if the animal had not been "altered." Who knew what visits to the vet might cost? We were already spending at least fifty dollars a year on a perfectly healthy cat. Dog food now cost about forty-five cents a can; two cans a day, three hundred and sixty-five days a year, totaled about three hundred and thirty dollars. And if the dog were ever caught off our property and without a leash, the fine would be twenty dollars for the first offense and would increase at twenty-dollar intervals for subsequent violations.

Back in the fifties, when we didn't even lock our doors, it never occurred to me to think of my dogs as crime deterrents. Now, most of the dogs in our neighborhood are primarily backyard security systems. Their relationship with the family is strictly business. The local police chief told me, however, that burglars actually fear house dogs like Chihuahuas and poodles as much as Dobermans and German shepherds. Apparently the larger, well-trained dogs often cower when given a strong reprimand, even by a stranger. The miniatures yap incessantly and are difficult to catch.

Thirty-five years ago dogs were undoubtedly more important sources of entertainment for children. Without television or air conditioning, we had more hours to while away outside. Because there was so little concern then about animal overpopulation, much of what we knew about birth, death, sex, and violence came from observing our dogs.

Every day this week the neighborhood children had

been drawn to Rosie like iron to a magnet, but many of them had dogs of their own whose newness had worn off and who remained confined in backyards with only an occasional garbage truck rumbling down the alley for entertainment. If Rosie stayed with us, would she be abandoned by the boys in six months like last year's electronic football game? I didn't think so. Drew had wanted a dog as long as I could remember. For years he has come to the dinner table with muddy paw prints on his body. Dog saliva doesn't leave much of a trace, but from having seen him in action I know that his idea of ecstasy is a kiss from a dog. For several years he considered becoming a veterinarian, but he recently decided against it. "I'd have to hurt 'em, Mom, to give 'em shots, and I just couldn't do it." He came home from a friend's house and said, "I just don't have enough animals in my life. I love it at Ralph's. The whole place smells like dogs."

On Thursday when I returned from an errand, Drew confessed, "I let Rose in, just a little bit, Mom." I tried to be stern, explaining that his grandmother might repossess the furniture she'd given us if she knew we were letting a dog have the run of the house. However, when a terrible electrical storm broke in the wee hours of the morning, I was up in a flash, like a mother with a newborn baby, to get Rosie in off the back porch. As I sat there drying and comforting this dog who really didn't seem the least bit disturbed by the storm, I resolved that if no one had claimed her by noon Friday I'd take her to the vet to start adoption proceedings. The timing would be perfect. The boys could spend their first week out of school building a doghouse with the wood craftsman next door.

"It's going to be the best summer we've ever had," I said as Drew and Jack left for their last day at school. But before I closed the back screen door Barbara, my next-door neighbor, waved the classified section of the morning paper at me. "Seen the paper yet?"

There it was. "Small gold and white collie, Glencoe Park area. Reward offered." Glencoe Park? How could she have come all the way across the expressway? I thought of a dozen reasons why the dog couldn't fit this ad. But I knew I'd have to call.

Reluctantly, I dialed the phone. The owner described her perfectly, even noting that she'd just weaned pups without my mentioning it. Her name, he said, was Brandy. I wanted to correct him on that—it made her sound like a cocktail waitress in a disco—but her ears did perk up when I called the name. I asked the owner if he could let me keep her at least until school was out at three-thirty. He agreed. All day I composed for the boys noble speeches about loving and losing, then discarded them in favor of tears when they got home from school.

To my surprise the boys remained dry-eyed and disgustingly philosophical about the news. One little philistine even had the nerve to ask how much we might expect as a reward. They had taken seriously all my hypocritical warnings about not getting too attached to the dog. While I couldn't even look at her without getting choked up, they engaged her in a final game of catch in the front yard.

The young man came for the dog as promised at five o'clock. I hoped for a fleeting moment that she might snarl at him or that my sons might look so forlorn at her leaving that the owner would relent and let us keep her. Neither happened, of course. Far from being forlorn, the boys kissed the dog good-bye and were thoroughly pacified by the owner's promise of a pup from her next litter. Maybe we'll go ahead with the fence and the doghouse. Little boys obviously don't learn enough about loving and losing in a week.

2 And What Exactly Is a Joist?

IT OCCURRED to me not too long ago that if my house were written up in a shelter magazine the writer's skill with euphemisms would be severely taxed. "Personal statements abound in this lively household. Even in the entry hall, one can sense the eclecticism that pervades the Mackintosh life style. On a small table a witty assemblage of a single tennis shoe, two Magic Markers, and junk mail from Kroger's welcomes you into the center hall, where distinctive handprints on the walls beckon you over the reclining long-haired puppy and up the stairway. . . ."

While I am not averse to pleasant surroundings, I am by birth or upbringing largely oblivious to what makes certain environments so pleasing. I married a man with a better eye, but we are both what I call adapters. We rarely evaluate the efficiency or comfort of our living patterns. A friend took one look at the straight-backed, hard-bottomed chair in which I've typed for ten years and said, "No wonder you haven't written lately!" The fact is, we don't even own a comfortable chair. I was glad she couldn't see my closet, with its rod designed for a six-foot-four man. I leap for my dresses every morning and have to drag in a footstool if a hanger gets caught. After sixteen

years of squinting to read at night, I finally put a lamp on
my side of the bed.

This unconscious adaptability served us well during our
student days. John and I stayed in Europe's cheapest ho-
tels with no complaints and survived some efficiency
apartments decorated in what must have been Early Airport. We even spent two years, while John went to law
school, living in one room of John's grandfather Porter's
small house in Austin, Texas. That experience has become
a barometer of our self-indulgence. In subsequent years,
as we became able to afford more spacious accommoda-
tions, we always half jokingly asked, "But could you go
back to Fred Porter's and be happy?" We could. We did it
this year.

Our son Jack has inherited none of our easy adaptability. In spirit he began our house remodeling project six
years ago by dragging home two-by-fours from a neighbor's building site to wall off his younger brother, Drew,
with whom he had always shared a room. After six years of
his lobbying, we decided it was time to convert the attic of
this old house into a bedroom and bath, which seemed
more economical and practical than adding on.

Many people who tackle a remodeling project save pictures from *Architectural Digest* and have a file on local
tradespeople and craftsmen who can transform their
dreams into reality. These people carry twelve-foot tape
measures in their pockets, and they are remarkably obser-
vant in the homes of their friends and acquaintances.
They are sizing up molding, door hardware, window trim,
and lighting treatments while I'm focusing on the chocolate soufflé on my plate. They communicate clearly with
carpenters and plumbers because they have mastered
definitions for words I only *thought* I knew, like "section,"
"elevation," "standards," "flashing," "studs," and

"valves." At our first meeting with the contractor, my husband started things off on an authoritative note by interrupting to ask the meaning of the word "joist." Above all, many people who undertake remodeling possess what I have long known that I lack—a certain supervisory presence that my husband sums up in the telling phrase "She could fire the maid."

My neighbor is much younger than I am, but she has all of the above-mentioned skills. I had watched her redo her own home, and I admired her ability to stand before a completed fence politely but firmly shaking her head and saying, "No, that's not what I wanted." I hired her to supervise my job in hopes that she would keep me from preparing fresh coffee for the workmen and soliciting their life stories. Surely in her presence I would be ashamed to confront errors with my usual dissembling "Oh, I hadn't realized that the new air conditioning wouldn't actually cool the new bedroom. Guess we'll just have to get some good fans, huh?" With my neighbor's eyes for plumb lines and quality work, a good architect's concept, and a terrific contractor, the job no longer looked so awesome. We gave the contractor the go-ahead and left for a two-week spring vacation, so that we would be out of the way as he began work and so that we wouldn't have to witness our house in shambles as an enormous hole was made in the attic.

Judging from the thick layer of plaster dust that covered every horizontal surface on our return, we had been wise to leave. A temporary stairway just outside my bedroom door led to a gaping hole, the entrance to what would be the third floor. The promise of new living space was exciting, but the gaping hole also said, "You've done it now. There's no going back." My husband, who reads too much about asbestos, was more concerned about the

fuzzy stuff floating down from the attic hole. He tied ban-
dannas over our noses the first night and commissioned
me to purchase painter's masks for everybody the next
day. By the second night back, we were so dry in the
throat and stuffy in the head that we knew we couldn't
stay in the house. It was time to go back, figuratively
speaking, to Fred Porter's. The place this time was my
eleven-by-twenty-foot office, which had been a storeroom
off the garage—only now we had three sons and a Christmas puppy from Brandy's litter.

While the boys were in school, I reluctantly hauled mattresses out to the office. By jamming my typewriter table
and straight-backed chair up against my desk, I could
barely fit four mattresses and one sleeping bag on the
floor. (The dog, I decided, would just have to risk emphy-
sema in the kitchen of the main house.) This little room
has an adequate bathroom, an efficient gas heater, and a
window air conditioner with a hum that will lull the most
inveterate insomniac. The room has never been as invio-
lable as I intended, but as I looked at the mattresses made
up on the floor, I knew that my tranquil hideout was about
to become a trampoline.

The first few nights required spankings to get every boy
confined to his appointed mattress, but after that we settled into a cozy routine rather like camping out. Since the
overhead light had to be turned out for everybody at the
same time, I pacified the chagrined older boys by reading
aloud from favorite books about bad children until my
throat was sore. After lights-out, the unfamiliar night
sounds began—not just the rattling of the garbage cans by
raccoons but also the night noises of our own children.
That sleep-robbing rustle of Pampers when they were
babies was nothing compared with the sonata they now
perform. One grinds his teeth a little, the youngest giggles

out loud at dreams he can never remember, and the third plays his adenoids arrhythmically.

I can't remember how many weeks we camped out in the office. Enough that it became routine and I found the confinement of everyone's clutter to a single room to be rather efficient. We still used the kitchen of the main house, but every other room remained dusty but orderly for the longest stretch since we had moved in. More than once we conjectured what it would be like to stay in the little office and lease the big house until we paid off the enormous debt we were incurring.

The initial progress on the remodeling was deceptively swift. Air-conditioning people worked miracles, snaking ductwork over ceiling beams just inside the eaves of the attic. Plumbers and electricians arrived on schedule and went about their work so efficiently that we began smugly to believe that the contractor had overestimated the time this project would take. Every day something new seemed to happen in the attic, and our enthusiasm easily overcame any discomfort we felt in our camping out. I prided myself on being able to monitor the work in the attic just by listening to the radio stations that blared from the third floor. The master carpenter chose classical music; the air conditioning crew preferred acid rock; the tape-and-float man always tuned in gasping evangelists. Before he left, he knowingly inscribed one untextured wall with "Jesus Save Them with Your Grace."

Some of the novelty began to wear off as we moved into summer. A nail driven into a water pipe drenched the first-floor breakfast room, and the carefully snaked air conditioning seemed capable only of bringing the attic temperature down to ninety degrees, thus requiring more Big Gulp breaks for the workmen. Out back, the ceiling of our encampment started to leak after it rained and required an unexpected expenditure for reroofing the entire garage.

I commiserated with a good friend who had been without her kitchen since January. "Sometimes my husband calls home and says he'll be a little late," she said. "I know he's running off to Spokane with some hatcheck girl, and I can't blame him."

I knew what she meant. Sometimes the tension so permeated the air that John and I lay side by side in our bed at night careful not to touch for fear of eliciting more incendiary remarks that would give us yet another night of sleepless hoo-hahs. At the brush of an elbow the tired and impoverished lawyer was likely to cross-examine: "You're sure they closed up that hole in the chimney before they Sheetrocked over it? Did they tell you they did, or did you watch them do it? . . . Couldn't you get them to make those windows they cut in the roof today just a little smaller?" Worst of all was the heavy sigh, accompanied invariably by "I sure hope we haven't spent all of this money to just screw up a perfectly nice house."

By midsummer I had no confidence about what we were doing. A Korean man sent to repair the air conditioning problem explained to me that "drain no can drain up." The toilet I had purchased well in advance was the wrong size. A custom-milled window promised daily in June arrived two weeks before school started. We could never locate painters on Monday morning and they usually disappeared by noon on Friday. My good neighbor, the supervisor, deserted the project to have her first baby. My children and even the dog became so accustomed to having strangers in the house that frequently when I was in the shower they would admit people who easily could have been typecast for *Deliverance*.

Only the contractor and the master carpenter sustained

me. Those two seemed to have enough skills between them to finish the project if all others failed. Like men of an earlier age, of a different work ethic, they solved problems that other tradesmen found insurmountable. I would like to apprentice my sons to them.

The window came at last, and the crude stairway was meticulously replaced with one whose balustrade matches the 1928 original that runs from the first floor. Carpet installers began to make the place like somebody's home. Eager to settle in, Jack and I hurdled the yet-to-be-installed stairway carpeting to move his bed and desk to the third floor. After lights-out, John and I were dismayed to hear him creep downstairs. "You're gonna kill me for this," he said, "but could I just sleep on the floor in Drew's room? It's weird being up there all alone."

3 *Free Agent*

IN 1963 Jack's Party Pictures on the Drag at the University of Texas in Austin displayed in its window a picture of me being embraced by UT football player Diron Talbert at a fraternity party. Actually Diron, who later played tackle for the Washington Redskins, is embracing a whole lot of people in this picture. His arms are very long. I just happened to be standing next to him when he felt the urge to give us all a big hug. Nevertheless, my husband delights in pulling the photo out during Redskins games to show his sons the caliber of men he surpassed to win my hand. The fact is, I never even had a date with Talbert; I had outgrown my love for football players in junior high.

Our son Jack was only about eight years old when a generous neighbor cleaned out her sons' closets and brought me a pile of their outgrown clothes, including a complete set of very small football gear—shoulder pads, helmet, practice jerseys—the works. I received it all gratefully but tossed the football stuff in a sack in my closet labeled "Next Garage Sale." Poor Nancy, I thought, her boys were just old enough to have missed the dawning of the new age—soccer. No longer would mothers have to sacrifice their sons' knees and shoulders to the gridiron.

Even better, soccer was a sport seemingly free of parental pressure. Nobody's dad had ever played soccer.

I should have known, though, that ignorance about soccer would be no deterrent to competitive parents. As early as 1976, organized soccer teams for four-year-olds began to spring up all over North Dallas. I wanted no part of them, however, and it wasn't until Jack was in the second grade that he started playing YMCA soccer. Y rules required "forced substitution" in each game, which meant that every kid got to play. Jack hated it. His team lost for most of the season, a phenomenon that he attributed to forced substitution, or, as he put it, "having to put the dorkiest guys in who can't even remember which end is our goal."

Despite his complaints, both Jack and Drew learned to play soccer well enough to maim my neighbor's crape myrtles and to keep my front yard free of St. Augustine grass. Most afternoons our yard was so full of little boys kicking balls between improvised goals that I wondered why anybody bothered with organized activity at all.

Nevertheless, the year Jack turned ten, the Y brochure proclaimed that soccer would not be offered for fifth-graders until spring. From now on, young man, fall would mean just one thing—*football.*

I felt relatively safe in leaving the Y announcement on Jack's desk. Some of his classmates had played organized football in the fourth grade, but he'd never expressed much interest beyond running out for a long one passed by his dad, collecting football cards from the neighborhood policemen, and reading Blackie Sherrod, a legendary Texas sportswriter. Well, come to think of it, one wall of his room was papered with Roger Staubach and Tony Dorsett posters.

At dinner that night he announced that he'd decided to

play football . . . sort of. He had some misgivings, he admitted, especially since many of the boys on the team had already played for a year. And he allowed that he was a little worried about getting hurt.

Mea culpa, there. I confess that I've read aloud or left obtrusively in my sons' paths every football horror story that has appeared in the daily paper—fatal heatstrokes, permanent paralysis, you name it. In fact, just that week I had torn from *Esquire* an eight-by-ten photograph of E. J. Holub's battle-scarred knees and was debating whether to mount it next to Tony or Roger in Jack's room.

To his credit, John remained very cool when Jack made his announcement, but he did fix me with a stare that said, "You butt out if this kid really wants to play." As the only female in the family, I frequently have to be reminded that little boys are more likely to base their self-esteem on their ability to throw and catch a pass than on their skill at writing a clever book report. John had played a little football in high school but, as I like to remind him, at his Episcopal school the lame, the halt, and the blind would have been suited up. Nevertheless, John maintains that his football experience was a valuable one, and he said he thought Jack ought to try it too. I acquiesced reluctantly, with the stipulation that if at any time he wanted to quit he'd get no flak from us.

Teams at the Y were impartially drawn out of a hat by the father-coaches. Jack's new coach called after the drawing to tell him who his teammates were and when the practices would be. He also told us where to get the necessary equipment. "He can have a number put on his jersey if he wants. My boy's gonna be wearing my old number, sixty-three," the coach said. That gave me a little shiver. Well, what did I expect in a coach—emotional detachment?

I waited until the last possible minute to buy Jack's gear. I kept thinking irrationally that whoever had bought that uniform at our garage sale two years ago would call and offer to return it. About an hour before the first practice Jack and I rushed to Oshman's sporting goods store to get him "loaded." As soon as the clerk laced the shoulder pads on, men from all over the store began to gather around us. "Going out for football, huh? First year? You're gonna love it," they said to Jack, who was already admiring what shoulder pads could do for a skinny ten-year-old frame. He disappeared into the dressing room to slip on the football pants. While he was gone some of the onlookers felt obliged to counsel me.

"Now listen," said one particularly stocky, bullnecked guy, "don't let that kid get into power building until he gets his full height on him. It can stunt your growth."

"And be sure he keeps his mouth guard in, even at practice," said another, displaying a partial plate.

When Jack reappeared with the white pants laced up, the clerk began showing me kidney pads, hip pads, knee pads, thigh pads. Never before had it occurred to me how ill equipped the human body is to play this sport. I braced myself for the sales pitch on helmets, knowing that clerks in sporting goods stores have a way of shaming frugal mothers into buying expensive equipment. This clerk was the rare exception. He passed over the fifty-dollar Riddell helmets, which didn't seem to fit Jack well, and selected a Wilson for nineteen-ninety. Jack was disheartened. The pros apparently wear Riddell. But I was gleeful. My friends had warned me that I wouldn't get out of the store for less than a hundred and twenty-five dollars and here I was writing a check for only sixty-five.

We raced home and tore off price tags. Jack's two brothers watched bug-eyed as he confidently laced the shoulder pads. Trying desperately to remember what went where, I stuffed the thigh pads, knee pads, and other pads into the pants. Then I helped him lace them up, briefly wondering if double knots would be babyish. He pulled on the huge white practice jersey, an open-weave garment so lacy that I couldn't resist humming the bridal chorus from *Lohengrin* as we descended the staircase. Although he was late for practice, I could hardly get him past the hall mirrors. He kept gritting his teeth and roaring through his face guard.

I thought he swaggered a little as we crossed the backyard to the garage. But perhaps that was the only way he could walk with all that padding. He climbed into the back seat of the car and pulled on his helmet. The kid next door, who is just young enough to hang on Jack's every word, stuck his head into the car to view the white splendor.

"Jack, did you get the kind of . . . kind of . . . cap you wanted?"

"Cap? Oh, my gosh, David, don't call it a cap. How many times do I have to tell you? It's a helmet. Naw, they didn't have a Riddell helmet to fit me."

When we got to the practice field I immediately noted that every kid was sporting the status helmet. And the entire team immediately noted that Jack was wearing his thigh pads on his knees. I took full credit for that faux pas and looked around for a convenient place for him to change. The back of the station wagon was clearly too hot and probably inadequate for a ten-year-old's modesty. I opted for a friend's house across the street from the field. It was early enough in the afternoon that I didn't think her husband, an orthopedist adamantly opposed to violent sports, would be home. He answered the door, of course, and with no reproving stares graciously offered the powder room to my helmeted son.

"This equipment should have come with a valet," I said, struggling to get the padded pants off, restuffed, and back on Jack's nervous, sweaty body.

"I knew Dad should have suited me up the first time," he groaned.

While he ran back onto the field, I self-consciously made my confessions to the orthopedist. "This is over my dead body, Ken. John thinks kids this age benefit from team sports, and he thinks there's no harm in it."

"I think he's probably right," the orthopedist said, to my surprise. "I encouraged my boys to play football in the fifth and sixth grades while most of them were too small to really hurt each other. Then I forbade it when it became so competitive in the middle school. Now one of them loves cross-country running and the other is a basketball player."

"But what about the time football takes away from schoolwork?" I asked, trying to elicit some negative comment from the good doctor.

"At this age, Prudence, I'm not so sure that the football isn't more important," he said. I might have stayed to challenge him on that, but the coach was motioning for me to come over to the field.

"This helmet just won't do," the coach said. "See, it really doesn't fit him—too loose. He needs one like this." He knuckled one of the other kids on his shiny Riddell helmet.

"But the Riddell helmets didn't seem to fit Jack either," I retorted, stifling the urge to say that anybody who would pay fifty bucks for a ten-year-old's football helmet had surely played without one.

"Well," the coach said, "I got one in my trunk that he

can take to Doak Walker's shop to see if they can rearrange the padding to fit him. He can use it for the rest of practice today."

Capitulating, I spent the next afternoon at Doak Walker's. What kind of fool was I to think that a salesman would agree to jerry-rig an old helmet when he could force us to buy the fifty-dollar item? Sure enough, the clerk shrugged and shook his head at the old helmet. He reached behind him for the new one, and Jack grinned from ear to ear. After exhausting my meager arguments on the clerk's deaf ear and creating a minor scene when he calmly informed me that the face guard would be an extra twelve ninety-five, I lost my place in the cash register line while I contemplated the options. "That's okay, Mom," Jack kept saying, "I just won't play. I know it's too much money. I *could* mow yards every week to pay you back, though, if you'd please buy it." Feeling like an idiot, I put the helmet on MasterCard and exceeded the speed limit considerably to get Jack to practice on time.

I hung around the practice field awhile that afternoon just to see what went on. ("No other mothers do that," Jack said to me later. "Why didn't you just go home like everybody else's mom?") A group of fathers leaned over the fence, watching the teams of small gladiators scrimmage. Every time the ball was snapped, these grown men unconsciously emitted a sort of primordial grunt, "Hunh . . . hit 'em!"

"Awright, boys, I wanna see me some billy goats on that line this time," one self-styled coach instructed. "Parker, get your shirt adjusted up there. . . . Okay, okay, let's put your bonnets on 'em this time, heads up, heads up."

Occasionally a father would claim the coach's attention. "Harry, those two on this end are just passing like ships in the night. They're not even wrinkling each other's jerseys."

I left then, but Jack wasn't so lucky. The team continued to practice every afternoon from five o'clock to six-thirty. Jack dragged in each day so tired that he could hardly keep his head out of his plate during dinner. Once in a while he would murmur some stoic report on the practice: "I caught a pass today but got tackled. Got the breath knocked out and I couldn't move for about five minutes." After dinner he'd look longingly at his younger brothers running back out to play in the twilight while he trudged upstairs to tackle his unfinished homework and fall exhausted into bed.

The first big game was scheduled two weeks after practice had begun. Even though Jack knew he was second-string running back behind the fastest kid in the whole fifth grade, he still had trouble sleeping the night before the game. When he came down to breakfast wearing his helmet and reviewing his playbook, he and his dad greeted each other with a forearm shiver and the same grunts I had heard from the fathers hanging over the schoolyard fence.

At the game I was amazed at how well the boys played. I had no idea that ten-year-olds could execute sweeps and reverses. The teams were well matched, and although our star running back did seem invincible, the final score was a tie. Since many of the players, including Jack, had no numbers on their jerseys, I was never sure whether he got to play. However, he had dirt on his white pants when I saw him afterward, so I confidently said, "Good game, Jack."

That weekend I took all three boys to the barbershop. Jack flipped through a copy of *Texas Sports* while he waited his turn in the chair. "Mom," he said, holding up a full-page color portrait of Dallas Cowboy quarterback Danny White, "isn't this the guy you really wish you'd married?"

I don't know what happened the following Monday to change his mind, but Jack came home from practice that afternoon and announced that he wanted to quit. I figured that he was just tired, had been chewed out by the coach, or maybe had had his breath knocked out again. I fully expected to find him the next morning growling through his mouth guard at the bathroom mirror. He wasn't.

At breakfast he said he wanted to quit football because he couldn't keep up with his homework anymore and he was just tired of having no time to play. "But football *is* playtime," I said. "At least that's what it's supposed to be."

"Are you kidding, Mom? Football just means getting beat up every afternoon."

When Jack had left the table John shook his head. "He's not giving up this early. I know what probably happened. He just got roughed up a little and his first impulse is to run. That shouldn't be encouraged."

"But he's right about the homework," I argued. "He's been up every night until after ten o'clock, and he's always panicked about some assignment he forgot to do the night before. I swore I'd never do homework for any of my boys, and here I am trying to write an eight-line poem about Columbus before the tardy bell rings. And besides, it seems to me that it shows good judgment to flee from pain."

The discussion degenerated from there. True members of our own generation, here we were, discussing fifth-grade football as if it were some monumental crisis in our son's life. I almost choked when I heard myself yelling, "And you're just perpetuating a system that has been eating men up for years!" John must have sensed the absurdity too; at any rate, we both cooled down before he left for work.

Spending the school day with his teammates didn't change Jack's mind. Reluctantly, I went with him to talk to the coach at practice time. The boys were lined up for a team picture when we got there. "Hurry, Jack," the coach yelled, "the photographer's ready to go."

"I'm not playing anymore," Jack said.

"Well, son," the father-coach grinned, "you were doin' good, but you've got to want it."

Jack's school coach, who oversees the elementary school Y program, happened to overhear us. He came over and put his arm around Jack and said, "You know, Jack, you're such a good athlete, I was hoping we could save you for basketball and track." I silently resolved to buy another set of encyclopedias from that man.

That was four years ago. If this eldest son regrets the decision, he's never told me. Oh, he puts that shiny helmet on every now and then. And he did ask me if I'd take a picture of him in his uniform to send to his pen pal in England. "You know, Mom, they call soccer 'football' over there. I thought he'd like to see what real football players wear."

I came through my first brush with football remarkably unscathed. But don't come to my garage sale looking for a bargain on a Riddell helmet. We have two more "free agents" running "fullback draws" in the upstairs hall.

4 *Dollar Signs*

"HE'S PROBABLY real poor," one of my sons commented, pointing to the smiling monkey trainer pictured in a newspaper article about the state fair. "I mean, you can't just do monkeys and make much of a living, can you?"

It would never have occurred to me at age eleven to consider a monkey man's earning capacity. In fact, I probably would have been shocked to learn that he got paid at all for doing something that looked like so much fun. Are little girls today still dazzled by the sequin-spangled lady on the trapeze, or do they cynically calculate the cost of her high-risk insurance and decide that her take-home pay wouldn't support their polo shirt habit? Maybe childhood is never really innocent, but I do think preoccupation with money begins at an earlier age these days.

Money didn't run in my family. My dad was the editor of the daily newspaper in Texarkana, Texas, when salaries for newsmen were probably commensurate with those for monkey trainers. The rewards were not financial. We had one car and, thanks to a grandfather who had received some property in payment of legal fees during the Depression, a small house with one bathroom and no mortgage. While I'm sure I knew families who had less than we did, as well as people who had much more, I just don't think I sorted them out that way. Economic status was not a childhood concern.

The vacations that my family took were always trips to newspaper conventions in Washington, New York, or New Orleans. My mother, whose frugality is legend, never allowed us the luxury of breakfast in the hotel dining room. If there was a Walgreen's within walking distance, we had our eggs and toast at the soda fountain. My brother and I innocently accepted her way of doing things without ever thinking that we didn't eat in the hotel because we couldn't afford to. Money was of such little interest to me then that I'm not sure to this day whether we were poor or just "sensible."

I don't remember having any steady income myself as a child, although I did request an allowance of fifty cents a week when I was about eleven. Since the allowance was not my parents' idea, they were as haphazard about remembering to pay up as I am with my own kids. They gradually lost track of the bookkeeping and simply gave me a dollar when I went to the Paramount Theater on Sunday afternoon with my friends. The dollar was adequate for my ticket, a box of popcorn, and a cherry lime afterward at the Grim Hotel drugstore on State Line.

Madison Avenue had not yet perceived children as a significant market, and consequently we grew up with little awareness of status items. I don't remember longing for any article of clothing—except maybe a bra, about four years before I needed one. The only recreational spending I can recall was done at Kress, the five-and-ten on Broad Street. For a dime or less I could purchase a package of ten pink rubber babies. They were each about an inch long, with rather poorly defined features, but the appeal was the quantity. When I outgrew babies, there was, of course, the makeup counter. Sometimes my friends and I would spend a Saturday afternoon first sharing a banana split at Otto's drugstore on East Broad and then perusing the Tangee lipstick and Cutex nail polish at Kress. I was a nail biter then, so nail polish was a decidedly impractical purchase for me unless I also sprang for false fingernails. I knew that my parents would not approve of the plastic talons, but I was totally seduced by the promise of nails long enough for Revlon's Fire and Ice. Retiring to a friend's house with the contraband, I trimmed and filed the plastic pieces and infected my cuticles with globs of airplane glue. I never wore those vampish nails outside my friend's bedroom because, once I got them all glued on and painted, it was impossible to do anything except admire them. It was an early lesson in the folly of excessive female vanity worth at least the forty-nine cents it set me back.

It wasn't until I was a student at the University of Texas that I heard anyone defined by his possessions. Someone in the dorm was pointed out to me as the girl who had twenty-nine pairs of Pappagallo shoes. Maybe the whole world had been counting, and I had just never noticed.

But economic status *is* a concern of my sons' childhood, and they will tell you right away that we are poor. By the standards of my youth, they have a luxurious existence, but they are quick to point out that we do not have cable TV; a video recorder; more than one television set; a condo in Colorado; a ranch, farm, or lake house; a microwave oven; Atari or Intellivision; an Apple computer; or a sports car or recreational vehicle. They are exasperated and perhaps embarrassed that I don't long for these things the way they do.

"At least we weren't born girls," they sigh with relief.

"What difference would that have made?" I ask.

"You would have dressed us like leftovers," one says, and they giggle a little at the prospect of the "dorky" dresses I would have purchased. A leftover, I gather, is an untouchable who fails to wear designer skirts and jeans and who either did not hear or chose to ignore the middle-school jungle drums that decreed canvas espadrilles this fall. Too young to understand parody, these preadolescents read *The Official Preppy Handbook* as a guide to life.

I read a newspaper story a couple of years ago about students at a local high school who were falling asleep in class because they worked two consecutive jobs after school. They were working in fast-food restaurants, not to assist their families or to buy necessities but to be able to afford luxury items—new cars, designer clothes, fancy stereos. Given the choice between a TransAm and a college education, they preferred the car. The symbols no longer necessarily represent success or wealth. The only status they convey is one of immaturity, poor judgment, and low self-esteem.

Where do kids learn that they are more important than their clothes or their ten-speed bikes? How do I keep my sons from becoming the kind of people who count pairs of Pappagallo shoes? How many times do I have to explain that they can accept Will's hospitality only if they really like Will—not just his computer or his dog?

There are dollar signs on almost everything in our children's world. While we would like to blame the power of advertising, we have to admit that a lot of their mercenary interest is learned at home. Inflation has put us in the habit of lamenting the cost of everything. They overhear discussions of real estate prices and show no discretion in announcing to a casual acquaintance what houses in our neighborhood are selling for. They know that skiing vacations cost more than beach vacations. When their lawyer father returns triumphant from the courthouse, they fidget while he reviews his final argument for them. He wants them to understand that his job really does entail upholding truth or seeing that right prevails. But it is easier to answer the question they're waiting not so patiently to ask: "Get on with it, Dad. How much?"

Likewise, a working mother knows that it is easier to justify the time she spends at her job if it's an economic necessity. Once last summer when I was working on a story a lot harder than I ever had before, I was incapable of any extended conversation at the end of the day. "Why are you working so hard?" Drew asked. "Because I'm going to get paid a big pile of money," I lied. Later, when the story was finished, I tried to backtrack and explain to him that, while I get paid for what I do, I do it because I like to do it. Or rather, I like to have done it. And no fee that I've ever been paid could really compensate me for the time I've spent lying awake nights reflecting on my work. I think he thinks I'm a fool.

What do we want them to know about money? When they were very young and constantly bombarded by the hard-sell commercials surrounding "Captain Kangaroo," we prided ourselves on making them wary little consumers. "Rip-off" was a concept they grasped before first grade because of toys that failed to meet their expectations. I even got them a subscription to a children's consumer magazine called *Penny Power*. It did run good articles analyzing junk food and exposing poorly made or dangerous toys, but anyone who has ever subscribed to a consumer magazine knows that more news of what is in the marketplace, especially when coupled with unbiased information attesting to its quality, is likely to increase consumption. So what if my boys now know which electronic toy is the best buy? We never intended to buy one at all. And while instructing them in the art of consuming, we must accept the fact that they will inevitably ask the price of everything.

All that my sons know of the free enterprise system is what they've picked up at their lemonade stands. Last summer Drew casually yelled out the back door, "Hey, I'm gonna set up a lemonade stand after lunch." His entrepreneurial friend next door stole his idea, skipped lunch, and was well on his way to healthy profits before Drew even hauled his table up to the corner. A price war began between the stands, and Drew lost—partly because his little brother drank a good bit of his stock and partly because I'm the sort of mom who deducts overhead costs from lemonade stand profits.

I have forewarned Drew that if he intends to make big bucks someday he may have to overcome some genetic limitations. Our family's attempts at increasing our income other than by the sweat of our brows have seldom been successful. My husband thinks his financial future was foreshadowed one afternoon when he was drinking beer with some old high school friends at the Spanish Village in Austin. He was, at that time, a sophomore in college, and he had just cashed a ten-dollar check at Tower Drug for the weekend. One of his friends, an heir to a Panhandle fortune, said, "Mackintosh, I'll trade you all the money in my pocket for all the money in yours." Unwilling to risk his ten dollars, John missed out on five hundred.

My children have learned that mothers are arbitrary benefactors. I have vaguely linked the allowance to the chore of making their beds before they leave for school in the morning. Even if they have actually managed that chore, I still grind my teeth when they yell from the couch in front of the Saturday cartoons, "Hey, it's allowance day." I invariably respond, "And I'll pay you little sloths when the porch is swept and the fingerprints are off the glass panes on the front door."

Their allowances are none too generous, but nevertheless my boys seem able to accumulate enormous amounts of money. When I offered to pay four cents a pane for window washing, I had never counted the number of windowpanes in this house, and the neighbors are far too generous when they pay for lawn mowing. Suddenly Jack and Drew have forty dollars between them, and if they want to blow it all on Pac-Man or Space Invaders at a local arcade, how can I stop them? Right now, I stop them by saying no and listen to wails of "Unfair! It's *our* money." Then they back me into a corner: "What would you let us buy?"

"How about stamps for a stamp collection? A down payment on a violin?" I wisecrack, knowing full well that there is hardly anything their little hearts desire that I really want them to have. Where are the children who want the things advertised in the Metropolitan Museum children's catalog? I know my children's bad taste is probably fleeting, and the experts advise to let them make their own mistakes so that they'll learn. But their mistakes are so costly. They aren't buying forty-nine-cent false fingernails at the dime store; they want a plastic racetrack that costs forty-five dollars.

"Why don't they just save their money?" the grandparents want to know. The two older boys do have savings accounts. Drew adds to his rather regularly despite Jack's telling him that savings accounts don't keep pace with inflation. He also advises that, once Drew puts it in, I'll never let him take it out. He's right. I've never quite decided what Drew's saving for. John and I mumble something about a car or college when he presses us for an explanation. Those may have been realistic goals in my day, when a good used car could be had for two hundred dollars and room and board at a University of Texas dorm was about five hundred dollars a semester. I suppose that underlying my tightfistedness with my sons is a subconscious fear that, if they become too accustomed to a certain level of affluence and to instant gratification, leaving the nest will be too difficult. They won't leave.

I want my boys to learn a little self-denial, but more than that, I want them to develop a few interests that don't cost money or require elaborate gear, so they'll feel free to make educational choices and career decisions on some basis other than "Will it pay?" Certainly, having enough money cuts down on many of life's frustrations, and being able to go out to dinner is preferable to eating Beanee Weenees. But I want my sons to know that it's important to learn things that have nothing to do with making a living.

In spite of all the consumer training we inflict on these boys and the self-denial we try to make them learn, we also wish for them a certain generosity of spirit that we admire in special friends, a generosity that has nothing to do with their economic status—it's just their habit of living with hands open instead of fists clenched, a knack for knowing when not to count the cost. Those of us reared in the shadow of the Depression don't come by that easily.

One evening this fall the five of us and a visiting grandmother went to the state fair. I have never anticipated the fair with anything but dread, since it has always meant spilled snow cones, runaway balloons, terrifying midway rides, and three tired, crying (or at least disgruntled), junk-food-filled children. But this year was different. After we ate the obligatory corny dogs, John did the midway duty while Grandmother and I took in the exhibits. When we regrouped at seven-thirty, everybody was still in good shape. We went to the automobile show and emerged just as the spectacular fireworks display began. Sitting on the lagoon steps, we watched the man-made stars spill out of the sky with breathtaking precision. William ducked his head slightly every time, since the fiery comets seemed to rain right on our heads. I said, "The big ones look like huge chrysanthemums exploding, don't they?" Jack and Drew said, "No, it looks like Vietnam." At least we agreed it was something oriental, and none of us could suppress the "oohs" at every new explosion. After a little wurst at Hans Mueller's tent, we departed the fair with a big bag of saltwater taffy and a pleasant sense of having enjoyed each other's company—the feeling that romantic mothers believe families are supposed to have all the time, but in reality happens so rarely. Before we got the last door of the car shut, one child shattered the moment: "What did that cost us, Dad?"

Who was counting?

5   *The Myth of Quality Time*

"I'LL BET you spend a lot of quality time with your children," a young mother said to me as we both browsed among the new stock in my favorite children's bookstore. She had that earnest expression I often see in mothers who have only one child and who are bent on perfection in their motherly duties. She had read a review of Christmas books for children that I had written and was intent on getting her child to sit still before Christmas for all twenty of the books I'd mentioned.

I assured her that reading aloud to my sons in December was an effective antidote to the breathless rat race we sometimes mistake for Christmas, but I hastened to warn her that it was no surefire route to cozy, romantic, meaningful moments with your children.

When William entered the first grade I spent the first days of my "liberation" perusing the ragged spiral notebooks and hardback journals in which I've sporadically recorded the past thirteen years. I was searching for "quality time." Instead I found a disorderly kaleidoscopic tale of high hopes, rocking chairs, runny noses, loose diapers, loose teeth, Oz books, earaches, music lessons, chicken pox nightmares, tough talk, interrupted sleep, chalk rocks, spear grass, broken windowpanes, hamster funerals, convulsive laughter and utterly irrational behavior by both adults and children.

"Quality time" at our house is a relative matter. The quality is only apparent when viewed against vast stretches of *quantity* time in which I question whether or not my sons have souls or even a normal range of human emotion or intelligence. Boys are not inclined to sit around chatting about life with their mothers, and mine are as suspicious of my planned family activities as they are of unprocessed nutritionally sound food.

I remember reading Letty Pogrebin's book, *Getting Yours*, about seven years ago, and being utterly awed by her suggestions to working mothers. Rather than emulating television fantasy mothers who exist to "service" their children by baking brownies and hemming prom dresses, the indefatigable Ms. Pogrebin suggested, "We might prefer to come home from the office and take everyone out for a bike ride or a jog through the park. Nothing beats a game of Scrabble before supper—unless it's calisthenics on the living-room rug."

Baking brownies? Hemming dresses? Scrabble? Was she talking about the "suicide hour" between five and seven when grease is popping in the skillet and a telephone computer is calling to congratulate me on having won a sweepstakes prize? Who needs a jog through the park when William is racing the yapping dog on a track that runs from kitchen to living room to dining room and ends with the dog skidding between my legs on the vinyl kitchen floor? We can't do calisthenics on the living-room rug; Jack wants me to explain nonrestrictive clauses again. And where is Drew? He's supposed to be at the piano practicing "The Ballad of Don Quixote" (also known as "The D. Q. Dude"), but I see him disappearing upstairs with contraband graham crackers. We've had some quality moments awaiting tetanus shots in doctors' examination rooms or perhaps in rocking chairs at 2 A.M. after nightmares, but they're seldom orchestrated, and they *never* happen between five and seven in the evening.

My middle son usually asks his philosophical questions before breakfast when I'm too groggy to be very articulate. Sometimes I only *think* he's asking a philosophical question. I gave him a whole treatise on the folly of war one morning only to find out he had asked me about a *wart.* Not long ago, however, he plopped down on the kitchen heater vent to finish dressing for school and asked, "Mom, why do the girls in my class cry so much?"

"Well, maybe they cry because they're more sensitive than you are. I don't know if it's the way society conditions females or not, but I do know my friend Susan's daughters are remarkably thoughtful. Did you know that Lee once set her alarm clock an hour early and ironed Rebecca's Sunday dress because she knew how much her sister likes to sleep and hated to see her get in trouble?"

"And that made her sister cry?" he asked.

"No, airhead, the point I'm making is that people who are sensitive to other people's feelings may also get their own feelings hurt more easily."

"Feelings . . . You never did tell me where feelings are," he said.

"Feelings? Well, they're in your heart, in your head . . . you know."

William had joined us by this time. Rubbing his not quite opened eyes, he interjected, "I thought you said they were in your teeth. You know, fillings."

Was that a quality moment?

We usually fare even worse with planned outings. Children are supposed to be eager for time alone with their busy fathers, but how many times have I seen the dirty station wagon roll in from a fishing trip with three disgruntled, ungrateful children. "I hate Dad. He made us have a snipe hunt, and I'm never going fishing with him again," one growls as they drag the fishing gear to the garage. The visits to museums, the weekend in the country, the Great American Vacation from which no one seems to remember a thing except "the souvenir shop where you wouldn't let me buy a peppermint patty" are, with few exceptions, all relegated to that vast area of childhood known as "Someday you'll be glad we did this."

When I reflect on all my years of mothering, however, it's the ordinary intimacies that I still find the most miraculous. Because we've spent quantity time together, I can sometimes read fatigue in their eyes and discount irrational tantrums. I have developed thermometer hands and can spot a before-school "fever faker" and dispatch him before the tardy bell. I am no longer shaken by the school's standardized test results. The child whose test indicated that he had difficulty locating shapes within a maze of other shapes is the one with whom I've worked 500-piece jigsaw puzzles. He can also find my car keys when I can't. Shapes within shapes indeed! Anyone who can wiggle his eyebrows like Groucho Marx and recite a whole Steve Martin monologue at age six is not likely to be very serious about standardized tests. The child who had a prodigy-perfect score in spelling labeled a map last night with "St. Lorans River" and couldn't spell his grandparents' last name. With three sons, I have learned to be patient when it comes to signs of intellectual achievement. The pretentious preschool that had my sons painting under tables flat on their backs so that they might understand and appreciate Michelangelo's Sistine Chapel failed to impress me. Just let their preschool diploma record achievement in shoe tying and independent toilet performance and I am totally satisfied.

I am also content with less than textbook mothering now. With my first two sons, I tried to make them reach every developmental milestone exactly on schedule. But my pediatrician only had two children. When my third was born, I told him he could no longer intimidate me. This baby gave up his bottle when the noise level of the other two abated sufficiently to risk unplugging son number three.

In these years, three sons have taught me to tolerate frustration, to develop patience, and to be incredibly flexible, all skills I hope they're learning too. The full-length jeans we bought for them two weeks ago reveal their ankles today, and I lie awake wishing the growth of my sons' grateful hearts could keep pace with their feet.

There will never be another time when I can observe so closely the mysterious and unpredictable changes that occur as little boys grow up. Quantity time, in that case, has its own inherent "quality." For example, my long-running performance as the tooth fairy only closed last week.

William discovered his first wiggly tooth while slithering down a water slide on South Padre Island last summer. In the two weeks he wiggled it, we talked exhaustively about teeth. He examined our sheep dog's teeth and searched photo albums for pictures of his brothers with big gaps in their grins. He looked at my teeth and marveled that the ones in front had known me as a first grader. "Did you ever wear 'bracelets' on your teeth like Anna [the baby-sitter]?" he wanted to know. "Tell me about losing your first tooth." All three boys are fascinated by my somewhat exaggerated tales of my stern mother who wielded a mean hairbrush in the fifties but who appears in their childhood only with "double-stuff Oreos."

"Well, you know your grandmother Ruth never tolerated procrastination in any form. Loose teeth were to be pulled as soon as possible. She usually knotted a long thread tightly around the tooth as soon as she saw me wiggle it. That left me with the option of letting her pull it out or going to school with that silly thread hanging out of my mouth."

William wanted more tooth stories, so we recalled the year Drew almost lost a dangling tooth in the communion cup at church. Drew remembered the time we lost his first tooth, really lost it, and we had to fashion one from a chicken bone to fool the fairy. Jack was embarrassed that I remembered his leaving a note to the tooth fairy asking for flying lessons instead of money. Drew remembered sleeping with his toothbrush under his pillow because somebody at school told him it would make his teeth get loose.

Everywhere we went, William displayed his wobbly tooth and we collected an assortment of tooth-pulling methods and fairy folklore from grocery checkers, neighbors and shoe clerks.

The tooth hung on precariously through the first two days of school. William's tongue developed a blister from the constant wiggling. On Wednesday night, after what may be my final reading of *The Waddle-I-Doers* from Betty MacDonald's Mrs. Piggle-Wiggle series, we decided to try the wet washcloth method on the tooth. "I won't pull it. I just want to see if I can get a grip on it," I promised. I gripped it all right. William's blue eyes widened as he thrust his tongue into the first vacant space. "It's gone," he squealed, trembling with a sort of wonder that I don't remember in his brothers. Then came the blood, the spitting, the cradling of the tooth, the attempts to reattach it and reenact the extraction, then the giggling, wiggling phone conversation with his father, who was away on business.

"Big deal," groaned his brothers. Okay, you had to be there and perhaps be his mother to know that this was more than a tooth pulling. This last little boy teeters on the seesaw of belief and disbelief when it comes to childhood fantasies. Cynical older brothers have left him very little magic.

When I tucked William in bed after the tooth pulling, we deliberated on the placement of the tooth. "I wanna keep it tight in my hand, so I can feel the fairy's wings," he said. Then he looked me in the eye and said, "Aw, but you're the fairy . . . aren't you? It's all fake. I know it's fake. . . ." He averted his eyes before I could confirm or deny his speculation. Then, sighing and rolling his eyes up toward the E.T. stickers on his top bunk, he said, "Mom, what do you think fairies do with the teeth?"

"Oh, maybe baby teeth are fairy money," I said. "With a first tooth, maybe a fairy can buy a silver-spangled gown, a new wand; maybe a toadstool sofa or a cobweb hammock . . ." He was asleep before I completed the fairy's shopping list.

Early the next morning, after depositing the fairy's generous gift in his bank, William started in again. "You never tell me the truth. There is no fairy. You put that money there. You're the fairy," he said, stopping to grin nervously and stick his tongue in the wonderful space.

"Maybe you're right. Maybe mothers are granted magical powers when their children lose teeth," I suggested, flapping my elbows.

"Show me that tooth, Mother," he insisted, "show me that tooth. I'm gonna take it to show and tell at school."

Reluctantly, I took him back upstairs and opened the small desk drawer where I had tossed his tooth the night before. He held the tiny white peg up to the light, rolled it once again between his thumb and forefinger, and tears ran down his freckled cheeks. "Faker, faker, faker," he yelled at me over his shoulder as he wiped his eyes with a sleeve and bolted downstairs to catch up with his brothers leaving for school.

Weeks later, when he reads his first book aloud to me, I tell him that we'll keep this *Drummer Hoff* book and someday he'll read it to his little children, and maybe they'll read it to their little children. "Oh no, stop," he says with a cosmic look on his face. "Is this the beginning? No, no, it isn't . . . You had a mother and she had a mother . . . Oh no, it's been going on forever and I didn't know. . . ."

My life with these sons is a curious mixture of violence and loveliness, of music and, more often, total insensitivity. I am dumfounded much of the time. For every one minute of normal conversation at the dinner table we have ten of cartoon imitations, rock lyrics or "Ernkh!"— the sound their school computer must make when they record a wrong answer. They ask what I'd like for my birthday and before I can give an answer they've decided that I'd probably like "three-piece cranks for Drew's bike" so I won't have to hear him whine about it anymore. Then they talk about worries. They conclude that the dog and I have no worries. William says he worries about first grade, Jack says he worries about stress. "I'll probably die before I'm thirty-five because I worry so much," he says. Laid-back second son can't think of a single worry. "Won't you freak when your parents die, Mom?" Jack asks.

"Yes, I'll probably freak," I reply.

"I know I'd freak if you died," he says. They all agree to "freak" at my demise.

The clod who baited his brother at the dinner table is sometimes a poet by bedtime. I don't know how to measure the quality of the morning that I drank my third cup of coffee with a naked three-year-old on my lap. He had strawberry jelly on one earlobe and dangled a link of sausage from his mouth, Bogey style. He was certainly good company and, like the small boy who believed in the tooth fairy in September, I never saw him again.

6 Cycles

JACK WANTS a motorcycle. This is no teenage aberration. It's an obsession that appeared from nowhere years ago. I have home movies of this child as a toddler, stomping his tiny foot on an imaginary pedal and extending his fingers to handlebar throttles. In his crib at night, he cuddled no teddy bears, soft blankets or pacifiers. He wanted tools— real ones. I permitted him to sleep with a small red toy screwdriver. "My quire! My quire!" he'd scream in the middle of the night, and either John or I would bound out of bed to search the floor around the crib for the wooden toy that had slipped from his chubby fist.

He collected and carried in his pockets the wheel pieces to any jigsaw puzzles that contained vehicles. He admired the crinkle-cut potatoes on his plate because they had "treads." I ignored his pleas for a plastic Big Wheel tricycle because it looked too much like a motorcycle. I bought him a nice red wagon instead. He still complains about the Christmas I kept Santa from delivering a toy known as the Evel Knievel stunt cycle. I thought this obsession needed no encouragement.

He strokes cycles in parking lots, buys magazines and posters that feature cycles performing daring feats and

never fails to point out make and model when we over-
take one on the highway. He raises the topic nightly in
hopes of wearing us down.

I respond with horror stories from my stint as a volunteer in the emergency room of the county hospital. "Give
your son a motorcycle for his last birthday" warned the
poster in the trauma unit.

But Jack has thought of every angle. "The best Christmas deal," he says to Drew, "is divorced parents." He has
surveyed the neighborhood and discovered that motorized two-wheelers are often the extravagant gifts given by
weekend fathers or sympathetic grandparents. "Mom,
aren't you and Dad arguing more these days?" he asks
hopefully. I think he's being facetious. However, at fourteen, this boy would sell his birthright for a Kawasaki KX
80.

I know he has ridden friends' mopeds on vacant lots
without my permission. On one crazy vacation, he has
ridden a moped *with* my permission. John promised Jack
for almost a year that, on our spring vacation in Mexico,
he, Jack and Drew would tour the fishing village of Isla
Mujeres on motorized bikes. When a complicated trial
kept John from making the trip, two hearts sank. Jack's,
because he feared the Yucatan with Mom alone would
mean museums and Mayan ruins, not mopeds. Mine, because I knew I couldn't disappoint him. I did, however,
harbor some hope that taking along his best friend Greg
and snorkeling the Garrafón Reef would make him forget
the mopeds.

However, by the second day on the island I was striking
a deal in my pidgin Spanish for four shiny red mopeds.
William remained at the hotel with his grandmother.
Jack, Drew and Greg hopped on their rented bikes,
revved the engines and rode to the end of the street as if

they'd been riding such vehicles for years. I lingered for some instruction, *"Vaya con Dios, señora,"* then tried to catch up with the boys. I lurched, then roared down the street, ruining my sandal by dragging it on the pavement for security. After long years of automobile driving, I am constitutionally unable to shift gears with my foot and give gas with my hand. I was not exactly a quick study with the handbrakes and gears on my three-speed bicycle purchased at a garage sale four years ago. I must have looked like Mr. Toad careening wild-eyed toward my sons, who waited at the corner. Forgetting this was not my ancient Huffy bicycle, I grasped the throttle like a brake and crashed into the back of Drew's machine. The boys wrenched my hand off the throttle and the bucking machine died. Thoroughly shaken, I climbed off to survey the damages. The mopeds were fine. I had a deep blackening bruise on my thigh and the rubber sandal I had employed as a brake was destroyed as was my composure.

"Boys," I said, fighting tears, "I can't do this. I'm sorry, but I'll kill myself before we get to the next corner. And I can't let you take off unsupervised." I was avoiding Jack's eyes.

"You could ride on the back of mine, Mrs. Mackintosh," offered Jack's thirteen-year-old friend Greg.

Well, what other options did I have? I limped with my moped back to the rental stall where the obviously relieved proprietor dropped his rosary and refunded my money. My requests for *los yelmos* (helmets) were met with shrugs, so I retied the bandanna on my head, took leave of my senses and climbed on the back of Greg's bike. We were off. "Greg," I yelled, tightening my grip around his waist, "let's don't tell your mom about this." The speedometer was in kilometers and, since I couldn't pray and do math simultaneously, I only hoped we weren't

going as fast as it seemed. Road signs, once we left the
town, were scarce, but those I could read as we sped by
said CURVAS PELIGROSAS. "Dangerous curves ahead," I
shouted above the roar to my oblivious sons who were
trailing us. My spine was fused by the time we had trav-
eled the five miles to El Garrafón. "You were great,
Mom," Jack said. "Didn't you love it, just a little?" I don't
know when he's ever liked me so much.

Most of the time, however, this child knows he's picked
the wrong parents. He gloated and chalked up points for
his side when Bill and Susan, family friends our age,
pulled into our driveway on their own shiny Honda Night-
hawk 750's. "Mother," Jack asked sarcastically, "don't
they have good judgment? Are they trying to make or-
phans out of their children?" Susan and Bill have read
Pirsig's *Zen and the Art of Motorcycle Maintenance* and
are undoubtedly finding truth on the back roads between
Dallas and Jefferson. How can I explain it? Bill has always
been a coconspirator with my firstborn. Knowing my nutritional scruples and Jack's affinity for processed foods, he
never drops by without some totally synthetic confection
from the convenience store. "A house without a good
supply of Hostess Twinkies or Ding Dongs," Bill says, "is
not a home." I should have known the motorcycle appear-
ance was imminent. Jack is ready to begin adoption proceedings.

He's always been in the market for a dad with a proper
respect for ratchet wrenches. Jack's desire for a motorcycle is, in part, a boy's longing for speed, power and even
danger, but I can't ignore the fact that he is our most
technological son. I rely on him to set digital clocks and to
hook up video recorders. All of his electronic gear is kept
in its original boxes with instruction booklets which he's
actually read. When his bicycle was due for a thirty-day

checkup, he gave me a carefully printed list to give the man at the cycle shop:

1. Black cotton tape grips
2. Repair brakes and clean
3. Repair and clean gears
4. Clean and check cranks with freewheel
5. Use touch-up paint on chips on frame
6. Clean rims.

He'd be great at motorcycle maintenance. If he were better at math, I'd want him to be my airline pilot.

When he was twelve, Jack acquired an afternoon paper route in hopes of earning enough money to buy his own moped. He reasoned that his expanding route would eventually make the motorized vehicle a necessity. In the winter months the paper route, especially the weekend papers, which had to be thrown before 6 A.M., became a nightmare. We had no intention of waivering on the moped decision, but I've never admired his determination more than on the morning Jack and I did that route together.

Getting up at five o'clock on a Saturday in late November was miserable, but how many sunrises would I see with my taciturn Jack? His attempts to find a friend to throw his route while he camped in the Big Bend with his dad the following weekend had failed. I was the last resort, and he insisted that I practice with him before he left.

The temperature had dropped to freezing during the night, and we quietly sorted through the jumble of last year's mittens and gloves in the front hall drawer. Thoroughly bundled in ski jackets, we took off on our bicycles. Jack would never be seen with me on my rusty old Huffy with the flower basket strapped to its handlebars once the sun rose.

Since I had had no coffee, only the sharp cold air made me alert enough to notice how clear the sky was before the expressways nearby offered up their clouds of exhaust. I knew better than to point out constellations to my earnest business companion. His younger brothers might stop between second and third base to examine their own shadows, but this dutiful, firstborn son is seldom distracted from the task at hand. He rode ahead of me with the flashlight since neither of our bikes is equipped with a light.

The delivery truck had dumped his supply of Saturday papers four blocks from our house. Jack expertly ripped the plastic bands from the papers with a dangerous-looking hunting knife his dad had brought him from Montana. "This works great," he said, stuffing the weapon back in his coat pocket. The Saturday paper, I learned, had two sections, so we had to remove our mittens to fold and band the two together. Letting that cold air get to our hands was a big mistake. They were never warm again. I performed admirably on the folding, but Jack shook his head as I began to stuff the papers in his canvas newsboy bag.

"Nope," he said, shaking his head and dumping the papers I'd stuffed helter-skelter in the bag, "you've got to lay 'em in there real straight, or you'll have to make too many trips back to reload." I could see that his meticulous nature was well suited to this job.

Slinging the heavy bag over his shoulder, he pedaled down the dark street. I anchored our flashlight in my silly flower basket and tried to avoid the potholes. I hated for him to see that I couldn't ride my bike with no hands the way he always does. Back and forth across the dim street, he gracefully figure-eighted, using only his narrow hips and occasionally one hand to direct the bicycle. Thunk . . . thunk . . . thunk. Each of his papers landed squarely on the sidewalk near front steps. Not surprisingly, I throw like a girl, and I was glad he wouldn't be there the following weekend to see me toss a few straight up over my head and into the gutter.

I followed him, carefully noting which houses received a paper. Some were weekenders only. Some received the paper only Monday through Friday. How could this adolescent mind that, just two nights ago, had such trouble recalling the events leading to the Texas revolution hold these details about his customers so precisely in his head?

As we darted past one block where he had no subscribers, I couldn't resist pointing out the sliver of a winter moon which, as dawn began to break, became a dark rubber ball lighted on one side, perhaps by the flashlight in my flower basket. Predictably Jack said, "Don't have time to look at the moon, Mom, we gotta get these papers to Mockingbird Lane." We headed down the more heavily trafficked street. Cars with their early morning high beams blinded us and scared me as they sped past, ignoring the speed limit. I took to the sidewalk, and before my eyes readjusted I collided with a huge sheepdog being walked by its owner. Barely restrained, the dog snarled and lunged at me as I apologized and tried to right my overturned bike. The dog didn't actually bite me, but my bicycle did. The leg of my best wool Pierre Cardin pants, my warmest, was secure in the teeth of my sprocket wheel. Jack, embarrassed by the scene with the dog, rode quickly on to reload his canvas bag. I briefly pondered my options. I could drag the bicycle home on my left leg, or I could convert the trousers to pedal pushers.

With bits of wool still clinging to the chain, I caught up

with Jack. While he stacked the remaining papers in his bag, I was a litany of complaints. "I'd rather be in Siberia, Jack. What are you going to do when it snows? What if it rains? Forget the weather, how am I going to deliver a Sunday paper three times as big as this Saturday edition?" Jack said nothing, just staggered a little as he readjusted the bulky bag.

The cold air made my ears hurt. Even the mittens seemed only to trap the cold air around my numb fingers. This part of the route was nearer our house, and I speculated aloud that we might lighten our Sunday burden by delivering the Sunday paper in sections according to readers' tastes. "The Moerschels have a football player son. Let's toss them the front section and the sports. Heather never has time to shop, so we can dump all of the advertising junk out of hers. That young Parkland intern probably needs the comics. The Kidds are house hunting. They'll spend Sunday on the classifieds and can call me if they want the rest. Some people would probably pay extra for such streamlined service."

Jack was not impressed.

Route completed, we zipped down the middle of Hillcrest Avenue, which in another hour would be so busy that we would have been hugging the curb. At dawn, however, we were kings of the road. Unburdened by papers or further responsibility, Jack swerved in and out of circular driveways with both hands in his pockets. We were home by six-thirty. I was frozen, exhausted, but also inexplicably exhilarated. Jack locked his bike and in ten minutes my smooth-cheeked entrepreneur was asleep in his warm bed.

As I made the coffee, I thought about the few years that he and I have left under the same roof. The other two boys might cling to our nest, but this fiercely independent and often adversarial firstborn will not linger. He has a steadiness and perseverance with unpleasant tasks that even now assures him regular employment. I have watched him methodically section our lawn and rake an entire season of leaves from six pecan trees without a break. He is anxious to run free and promises to teach us a thing or two in his adult life. Our house is old and usually cluttered. His will be new and sparse and Japanese-efficient. I am content to drive a well-worn station wagon; he, of course, will have a shiny, perfectly maintained Kawasaki KX80.

If I don't suggest it, maybe he will at least wear a helmet.

7 *Generations*

"IT DOESN'T take me long to look at my grandchildren," my father has always said with tongue only partially in cheek. Known to his three obstreperous grandsons as J.Q., he gives himself no more than a low C as a grandfather, and I suspect gives my sons about the same grade as grandchildren.

I'm not wounded by that. He and I have long had a mutual admiration society and, quite frankly, my sons have been an enormous disruption in our ongoing affair for the past fourteen years. "When are you going to write about something besides those children?" my father asks, oblivious to the fact that, while I am talking to him, I have the telephone receiver cradled against my right shoulder so I can slap a small hand away from the chocolate chip cookies I just baked for the PTA and feed the dog, who is pathetically chewing my houseplant for nourishment. Even while I speak affirmatively to him about his latest newspaper column, I am shaking my head wildly at the teenager who says he's going to ride somebody's moped to the 7-Eleven.

Later, at dinner, it occurs to me that my sons don't even realize that their grandfather celebrated his seventy-sev-

enth birthday on Wednesday. I sent the letter and present. I didn't even have them sign a card. To assuage my
guilt, I announce to them at dinner, "Should anything
ever happen to me, will you all please remember that
your grandfather's birthday is Columbus Day?" In his
honor, I hold them at the table long enough to read his
Sunday newspaper column aloud.

The bond between grandchild and grandparents that
once must have grown with so little tending now seems to
require conscious effort. And, as a child who grew up
without grandparents, I hardly know where to start.
Grandparents seldom live in the same town with their
children, and even when they do there seems to be a gap
between my generation's experience and expectations
and the contemporary reality.

Part of the problem may be that our expectations are
colored by the storybook-movie-television romantic no-
tions about who grandparents should be. We envision
round, soft, gray-haired grandmothers with pies in the
oven at rustic farmhouses and grandpas who can hold
grandsons spellbound before a blazing hearth with tales of
ghosts or Indians. The reality is often startling. They live
in a condo. Grandmother has had a face lift, has nothing
but bran in her refrigerator, runs a profitable antique
shop, plays tennis three times a week and, while she'd
love to see the grandchildren, next week she's leaving for
China with a group from the church. Grandfathers still
look like grandpas, but many had little enough to do with
their own children growing up, and frankly would rather
play golf at the club or see the MacNeil/Lehrer report
uninterrupted by the ungrateful little scofflaws.

While our own real grandparents may not have fit the
storybook stereotypes either, in our memories we have
romanticized them and made them a little larger than

life. We have remembered selectively and perhaps been far more tolerant of their shortcomings than their own children were; because, bless them, they were often more tolerant of us. My husband remembers his grandfather as the one who taught him to fish and hunt. To his own children, however, he may be remembered as the father who made them eat too much fish and squirrel.

A friend speaking of her favorite grandmother recalls, "I can still see the way her eyes lit up when I entered the room. It didn't matter that I was a gawky teenager; I was her granddaughter and she adored me. She had a passion for music and never missed the Texaco radio broadcasts. She took me to every musical performance Beaumont, Texas, could attract. She introduced me to Patrice Munsel, Isaac Stern and Jascha Heifetz before they were internationally known stars. My teenage friends and I giggled all the way home from operas at Lamar Tech and mocked the melodramatic arias, but it was an exposure that took. Music is very important to me. Ninnie grew up in a small rural community, and she really envied my education. In fact, watching her pore over the college catalogues with such relish probably made me value the educational opportunities at Smith far more than I might have otherwise. She loved it when I moved to New York after college. She seemed so 'with it' even at eighty-four that when she came for a visit I got tickets to Edward Albee's *Who's Afraid of Virginia Woolf?* When the main character, Martha, bellowed, *'Screw you!'* Ninnie gulped a little but never said a word. After the play she said, 'Nancy, I thought the acting was really good, but I *am* puzzled as to why their boy never came home.' "

Another friend recalls that each Christmas a different grandchild in her family was given the position of honor beside Grandmother at the festive table. "When it came my turn, Granny whispered in my ear, 'I'm so glad it's your turn. You've always been my favorite grandchild, and I'll always love you the most. Don't tell the others, honey. It's our secret.' I probably glowed brighter than the candles on the table that year. Only at her funeral twenty years later did all of the grandchildren learn we'd all been told the same secret."

My own grandparents died before I knew them. Grandfather, for me, was only a stern-looking portrait of a bald man looking rather disapprovingly from the wall of my father's newspaper office. Grandmother, in a companion portrait, looks softer, but I am told she audibly corrected the Methodist minister from her pew on Sundays. Pictures and memories of my maternal grandparents were lost in a fire.

My great-aunt Mary Cox was the closest to a grandmother I knew as a child. My memories of her are mainly sensory ones. The sight of a canary or the taste of real butter on oven toast always transports me to her tiny kitchen on Blanton Street. My practical and thrifty mother was firmly committed to margarine, but "Coxie," who lived on a railroad widow's pension, never had less than the real thing on her table. At eighty, she was a tall, handsome woman whose erect Victorian posture I was encouraged to admire and emulate. Her hair was frizzy and blond, and her nails were always painted Windsor Rose, a color that never did much for my fat little fingers. Incongruously, she chain-smoked, read paperback novels which she always denounced as "trash" when she'd read the last page, and trounced me soundly at casino and canasta. She let me cheat a little on my "polio-preventative" naps. I got full credit if I lay quietly on a pallet in her living room while we listened to her radio soap operas. I remember her scolding me only once, when, without her permission, I took the small metal box from her closet to show a neighborhood friend all of her love letters, postcards, pictures and other mementos of her husband. For my birthday, her real butter went into heavy moist orange juice cakes which I've never been able to duplicate. She snored at night, and I always prayed fervently before climbing into her slopey feather bed that I'd fall asleep first. In the countless days I spent at her house, which was only five blocks from my own, I can't remember that we ever talked about her childhood or my mother as a little girl. Maybe I didn't listen. Coxie died after a lengthy illness in our home. In her last weeks she was frequently confused, and I was upset when she called me Emma. "That was her sister," my mother explained. I had never thought of Coxie having a sister or being a child herself. I once heard an eight-year-old say, "You know why grandparents are so nice? They never had any children." I suppose it's part of the egocentric nature of childhood that makes us believe our grandparents' lives began when we, their grandchildren, were born. Bless them for letting us believe it.

I had no grandfather figures in my life until I married. My husband's grandfather allowed us to share his house during John's law school days in Austin. While as a young bride I was eager for our total independence, they were, nonetheless, good days. During John's brief stint in the Army, I lived there alone with Papa Porter. Well into his eighties, Papa was still waking up with a long list of things he had to do. He had a garden to cultivate, roses to tend, and a bird dog to train. He was still driving ("aiming," we called it) his tanklike 1954 Chrysler to Academy Surplus for tools and fishing gear or to Culp's Super Foodland for some huge can of cling peaches on "special." In my very amateurish newlywed way, I cooked for him most eve-

nings, but long years of living alone made him most content with his own concoctions of canned tamales, TV din-
ners, Jell-O with fruit cocktail and cake-mix chocolate
cupcakes. Once when I had exhausted my cooking exper-
tise to produce "chicken diablo" with chili powder turn-
ing the sauce an unappetizing pink, he said in exasperation, "I don't see why you don't just fry it and make some
gravy. Everybody likes it that way." We had our domestic
disagreements from time to time. His untrainable bird
dog, Ginger, routinely ran through the neighborhood
with my bras off the clothesline, and when I washed the
dishes he claimed that I deliberately left the knives pok-
ing up the wrong way in the dish drainer. He frequently
left old coffee boiling away on the stove, but when we
cleaned up the kitchen together some winter evenings he
harmonized his cracked old Methodist tenor with my
Baptist alto, and we'd let her rip with "On Jordan's stormy
banks I stand and cast a wistful eye . . . I am bound for
the Promised La-a-a-nd."

Often when I came home from teaching school I'd find
a full-blown pink and yellow Peace rose in a jelly glass on
my desk. In his tobacco-sprinkled bed I might find a feverish neighborhood child who much preferred being sick at
Papa's, where she could watch the bountiful bird feeder
outside the bedroom window and eat as many stale
oatmeal cookies as she remembered to say "please" and
"thank you" for. After dinner, if the Houston Astros
weren't playing, he'd tell me stories about camp meetings
in Salado or about playing the clarinet in the Spanish-
American War in the Philippines. "Did any of your buddies marry Filipino girls?" I asked after he had described
how beautiful they were. "No," he shrugged. "You didn't
have to." When the stories ran out, he'd read me his

favorite jokes from the *Reader's Digest* or time me with a stopwatch on the Word Jumble from the afternoon paper.

After law school, when John and I moved to Dallas, Papa and his dog came to visit us on all holidays. As he approached ninety, we often butted heads over the thermostat at Christmas. Even with two flannel shirts and thermal underwear he was never warm, and basting a turkey in the kitchen, I was never cool. Sometimes, after feeding a baby at 2 A.M., I found him in the kitchen with a bottle of bourbon mixing up what he called a coffee royale to banish a terrible nightmare. The grandson who had fished and hunted with him as a child was now a harassed young lawyer and I was a tired young mother. We never again gave him the attention he deserved. He planted a garden at our house for two consecutive years and taught me to tie up the tomato plants with discarded panty hose. He mended my dime-store teapot and some beach sandals he found in the wastebasket. He chastised us for letting our bird feeder stand empty and boasted that his martin boxes were occupied every spring. My toddler sons adored him, and we treasure the home movie we have of him at ninety crabbing with them on Bob Hall pier in Corpus Christi.

Once, when he rode with me and my sons out Preston Road in Dallas, the traffic snarled to a standstill as motorcycle policemen with sirens blaring cut authoritatively through the line of cars to lead a funeral procession. Funeral was a new concept for my five-year-old, and in his exhilaration at seeing the motorcycles and sleek black limos he turned to his great-grandfather and blurted, "Papa, if you ever have one of those, you'd better invite me."

Being a grandfather was Papa's calling. He had all of the manual skills that fascinate young boys and a patient, accepting manner that made children and dogs his constant companions. Few grandparents are so gifted, nor do all grandparent-grandchild relationships blossom so naturally. Rivalry between generations can often be a barrier. As Selma Fraiberg wryly puts it in her book, *In Defense of Mothering,* "It is a beautiful tradition in North America that the wisdom of one generation should not obstruct the path of the next." That is, my grandmother, who breast-fed her babies, would probably think that a disgruntled child needed a purgative. Her husband believed that "a penny saved is a penny earned." My mother, who bottle-fed her babies at four-hour intervals, believed the back of a hairbrush routinely applied to our bottoms improved our attitudes, and their generation thought a penny invested in a U. S. Savings Bond was a penny earned. My contemporaries, breast feeders again, watch their offspring throw tantrums, feel guilty, and reach for yet another "How To" book. Our children don't believe pennies are real money. It's not a tradition that knits generations together.

A visiting grandmother sees her grandson come in shirtless from playing in the front yard. His baseball cap remains on his head while he eats his lunch on a paper plate at the "breakfast bar" where he consumes most of his meals. "I sometimes worry that my grandchildren are growing up 'common,'" she confides to a friend. The respectability her family clung to with cleanliness and impeccable manners in the Depression seems ironically to be dissolving in an affluent household too casual and indulgent for her taste.

As parents in the late sixties and early seventies we were encouraged by experts to embrace a whole new way of rearing children. We were to tend to our children's physical needs, sort out a rapidly shifting moral code, but most of all protect our children's emotional health. The job, we learned, also included monitoring television (the neighbor's cable), junk food, nitrites, dyslexia, pollution and child pornography. And five years into the overwhelming task, we mothers were advised that we could not count on a child to give reason and meaning to our lives. We needed a career.

What did our parents know? We didn't even have babies the same way. To assure our children's emotional stability from the very start, we were wide awake and panting for the delivery; our husbands were not only present in green scrub suits, they had cameras. Breast feeding versus bottle feeding was not a matter of nutrition or convenience. "Emotional bonding" was at stake. Even diapering a baby took on psychological significance. Any parent who expressed disgust on viewing the contents of a smelly diaper was guilty of fostering unhealthy attitudes toward normal bodily functions. To grimace or gag while cleaning a loose diaper load off a Tonka truck was to endanger our children's sex lives or, at the very least, give them hemorrhoids.

When my mother came for a visit with my firstborn, I winced to see her spank my baby to get him to lie still for diapering. "Why exhaust yourself and let him kick you in the face? A quick pop on the bottom will stun him long enough for you to get the pin fastened," she wisely counseled. "But what about his psyche?" my generation wailed.

So healthy was my oldest son's attitude toward his bodily functions that in desperation I dispatched him at two and a half to his spanking grandmother with the instructions: "Toilet-train him, and don't tell me how you did it. Just send him back in clean training pants." She did.

And when he sends me a bill for analysis someday, I'll forward it to her.

As young parents we were inundated with information on building children's self-esteem, nurturing creativity and intelligence and "mirroring feelings." Could we entrust our children occasionally to their grandparents, who belonged to the "straighten up and fly right" school, where healthy expression of feelings just might smack of impertinence and receive the hairbrush treatment?

A good friend confides: "My father's first question to my sons is always, 'Are you Number One?' He wants to know if they're at the head of their school classes and if they're on the winning soccer team and if there is anybody ahead of them and why. My father treated me that way too," she says, "as if, if we weren't Number One, he wouldn't love us. It makes high achievers all right, but the emotional price isn't worth it."

Still another mother worried that her child, who attended a thoroughly integrated school, might return from the weekend at Grandpa's saying "burr head" and "Meskin." "He's never going to change, but I don't want those narrow, racist views inflicted on my daughter."

Our instincts were protective, but what we underestimated was the incredible resilience of our children. While we worried about grandparents' intolerance, we overlooked an opportunity to develop some tolerance in our own children. Having the perspective of three generations, even if some of them seem cockeyed, is bound to make life a little richer.

The relationship between grandchild and grandparent is seldom rivalrous. The intervening generation acts as some sort of buffer, allowing Gran and the little knotheads to be benign coconspirators. "A grandmother is someone who never yells, 'Hurry up,'" says a third grader. "I have what their mother does not have," says that grandmother I met. "I have *time.*" Since her grandchildren were born, she has invited one to spend the night with her every weekend. "I just knew that my husband and I could enjoy them more, one at a time. I sometimes help my daughter by having them all, but it's not the same."

The day I talked with her, she had just mailed a buttermilk pound cake to a granddaughter who is now in college. Ten loaves of bread were rising in her kitchen as we spoke. "I knew that I wanted my grandchildren to be interesting people, and you can't be very interesting without a 'background.' 'Ponsie', as the children call my husband, and I are the background. We've taught them games, hard games that require thinking—not the stupid ones. They all play chess, Othello, dominoes, Russian bank, Yahtzee. Never Monopoly! I call it 'Monotony.' Oh, and Scrabble. Spelling's not very well taught in school these days, so we play a lot of Scrabble. As soon as my granddaughter learned enough French, we played Scrabble in French. We tell them funny stories about their mother and uncle growing up and stories about our own childhoods. We read aloud to them a lot. We started with *Winnie the Pooh* and through the years I think they've heard *Heidi, Little Women, Alice in Wonderland.* We've read all of Frank Baum's Oz books several times. We also inflict our travel slides on them. They have favorites that they'll look at over and over again. Before their family went to England last year, even the eight-year-old had some definite ideas about the things she wanted to see. Discipline is never a problem when we see them one at a time. And, you know, a grandparent usually only has to correct them once. Parents are the enemy to be outfoxed; not the grandparents."

Other grandparents I have talked with have developed

clever ways to be with their grandchildren. One arranged for her seventeen-year-old grandson to wash her car weekly. He's reached the age when going to Grandmother's seems a little childish, but the car washing gives him an excuse to drop by. "Perhaps I need him more than he needs me," she says, "but I can't help thinking that he enjoys this little shelter where the pressure is off."

Some of the grandparents I talked with had "rituals" their grandchildren will always remember. "Three o'clock is a good time for chocolate pudding, and my granddaughter knows if she's with me we'll have our pudding come hell or high water," says one wise grandfather.

The grandchildren I have talked with appreciate very specific things about their grandparents. Some remember glorious indulgent Christmas presents—whole Indian suits and tepees or "a silver teardrop from Tiffany's supposedly wept by a fairy when Grandmother couldn't come to my birthday." Some admit that Grandma's food was still the prime attraction. A younger child remembers, "Legos and puzzle pieces never get lost at my grandparents' the way they do at home. Things are always right where they're supposed to be." "Once a year, they let me get out all of my great-great-grandfather's Civil War medals and his gold spectacles. It's the neatest stuff. And sometimes my granddad tells me about Prohibition. It's so cool. He's also a great poker player." A college student reports that his date at the university recently complimented him on his manners. Apparently she seldom encounters boys who know how to open doors or pull out chairs in restaurants. "I just told her, 'I've got a grandmother in Del Rio who'd kick my butt if I didn't.' "

Such relationships require patience and time. The best grandparents seem to be the ones who have a clear sense of what they have to offer and who give it with both barrels. They pass on family stories, funny baby-talk words, stamp collections and train sets. More importantly, they give unconditional love and provide havens from pressured rivalrous environments.

The grandfather and the grandsons who rate themselves as C— may yet make an A. The groundwork is laid. It began in a rocking chair with "Kimo-nero-delsy-karo . . . ," a nonsense lullaby he sang to me and then to them. As toddlers, they asked about his stuttering and they bragged to friends that they had a granddaddy who could "speak in pieces." He told them that he was the world's greatest gin rummy player, so that when they beat him they thought they had a national title. Drew once returned from a Texarkana visit singing all the verses to "Please play for me that sweet melody called Doodle-dee-doo," but he still needs some coaching on "Oh, what a time we had with Minnie the Mermaid. . . ." They will giggle over J.Q.'s childhood story of his blowing a treasured quarter on a huge sack of beautiful but bitter cranberries as many times as he cares to tell it.

One at a time, they are not quite so obstreperous. We no longer believe that they are fragile, but as they approach these teenage years they need some strong allies whose judgment is not so "boring" or threatening. Besides, if J.Q. lets them drive his golf cart from time to time, maybe they'll lose interest in going to the 7-Eleven on the moped. Two of them might even sit still for MacNeil/Lehrer.

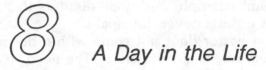

8 A Day in the Life

I'VE NEVER attended a time-management seminar, but I've read enough books and articles on the subject to conclude that such schemes have little to do with the life I lead. I have tried listing priorities and setting goals. I even have an indexed notebook, which I have left more times than I care to remember at the check-cashing window at Safeway. I balk, however, at the suggestion that I brown thirteen pounds of hamburger meat in my turkey roaster to make twelve freeze-ahead casseroles. Who are the children who eat Crunchy Hamburger Noodle Bake?

The regular ordering of my day comes when my attorney husband leaves the house at about eight-fifteen. His mind is already fixed firmly on a day that is divided on his desk calendar into hourly appointments. I have visited his office and seen little yellow pieces of paper lined up on his desk awaiting his disciplined and rarely interrupted dispatch. Briefcase in hand, he invariably turns as he goes out the door and says, as if dictating a memo, "If you have time today, could you do as follows: (a) get my blue pants at the cleaner's, (b) call about tennis lessons for Jack, (c) figure all the sales tax on the checks in last month's bank statement?"

I laugh and reply, "Moreover, by copy of this letter all other counsel of record will be provided a copy of the above. In addition, please add section (d): measure out life in coffee spoons." My day began two hours ago, and I can already recount triumphs and small disasters that time-management experts never anticipate.

My job as a writer does not come with a downtown office, a supervisor, or a time clock. The need to write hovers around the edges of my more insistent vocation—mothering. Daily, small people clamor at my elbow for clean socks, meals, mediation, lunch money, crazy eights and chauffeur service. Editors intrude less than once a month, and then only by long distance.

"There will be time—aeons of time—when your children are grown," says the internist who diagnoses my stress from time to time. He doesn't understand that in my case one vocation feeds the other. Although being the mother and the writer makes my life complicated and often inefficient, I want to write from experiences I'm having now. Children are not items on a list, to be scratched off when finished. They are never quite finished, and life with them must be appreciated in the process. Writing helps me step back and notice the process.

"I know you're writing every day," an artist-mother confides, "and I want to know how you do it, because I'm not painting." The doctor's promise that someday there will be time does not assuage her either. "The painting," she says, "it's like an itch in the middle of my back that I can't quite reach. And if I ignore it, postpone it, it becomes something that I'm not even sure I can do anymore." We both agree that playing Bach on the piano helps.

Most mothers caught up in the minutiae of life with small children have the frustrating illusion that in other houses mothers with more discipline who need less sleep are proceeding through a carefully balanced day full of uninterrupted intellectual pursuit that enables them to have a sense of real accomplishment. Somewhere, perhaps, but not here.

We stayed up far too late last night reviewing the characteristics of the phylum Echinodermata with Jack, our seventh grader. I was slaphappy by ten-thirty as we dramatized the weird defense mechanisms of the sea cucumber. The ultimate riposte: when attacked, the sea cucumber can eject its intestines into the face of its assailant. I don't remember having seventh-grade biology on my priority list, but it left no time to wash my hair. I set the alarm for six, hoping to shower before breakfast and perhaps to make notes on a magazine article I had outlined last November.

William awakens me five minutes before the alarm goes off. "Have I got a dream for you!" he announces. His father plays Academy Award possum, obviously relishing his favorite predawn fishing fantasy, which we call "Gone to Port O'Connor to Catch the Big One." I muzzle William (who has no whispering voice), forgo the shower, and head for the kitchen to make coffee before settling in for a play-by-play account of a witch who kidnaps William and his brothers, locking them in a room lined with stuffed animals that have laser eyes. One look at the snake's laser eyes and you turn into a stone deer. (Here I detect some mingling of Saturday morning cartoons and C. S. Lewis' *The Lion, the Witch and the Wardrobe.)* The dream, of course, has a heroic ending. The witch gives William a present that he instinctively knows is a bomb. He hurls it at the witch and all the stuffed animals and—*kaboooom!*—his brothers are saved.

Perhaps I am the witch. As Rosie the dog and I go out to

fetch the morning paper, I see that Drew has once again left his new bicycle unlocked in the yard. I note on the calendar when he'll be allowed to ride it again. Bookkeeping on the transgressions of three sons does get tedious.

At breakfast, which despite my best-laid plans is always served short-order style, I succeed in getting our almost adolescent to eat a scrambled egg. I never intended to become the sort of mother who nags about nutrition, but as other convictions are worn away it's comforting to know that my epitaph can still read: "She never bought presweetened cereals." Nevertheless, Jack's diet usually consists of cereal for breakfast, four Nutty Buddies for lunch in the school cafeteria (I don't know who eats the sandwich and apple he packs every morning), and who knows what contraband in the afternoon while I'm chauffeuring his brothers to soccer and music lessons. An egg and orange juice on a Monday morning represent a major triumph.

William ordinarily attends afternoon kindergarten, but today he has to rehearse with the morning class for the play the kindergarten is going to perform. As we dash to the school after his brothers have departed, I remember that Jack's gym clothes are still in the drier. Failure to suit up means he gets what the coach at middle school calls the palm leaf. "How we gonna teach your boys any responsibility if you keep lettin' 'em play you like a yo-yo, bringing those gym suits up here when they forget 'em?" the coach says to parents every year at open house. I don't know. I'm the mother who refuses to accept the laundry responsibility until late Sunday night when nobody has clean socks. I decide to let him take the palm-leaf paddling anyway. Duck wings and angel halos need adjusting in the kindergarten.

At the elementary school, costumed children are too

excited to follow instructions from any adult. The rehearsal is delayed because one small boy is cowering in the rest room. He is the only male duck and has just learned this morning that his costume is a yellow leotard with orange tights. I enter the boys' rest room with Sue, another mother of sons, to counsel with him. "I can't let anybody see me like this," he says, tears spilling down his cheeks. Sue and I, sympathetic to the fact that he has older brothers in the school, look at each other and agree, "No, he can't." I find his blue jeans in his locker, and when the time comes for Daddy Duck to summon his three little ducklings, no one seems to mind that beneath his wings he's wearing Levis.

After some minor footlight adjustments the rehearsal goes on. I take a seat in the auditorium and make a note to pick up camera film. This is my last baby's kindergarten show, and even though he has been cast as a rubber-tree plant, we'll join the rest of the fools with flash attachments tomorrow night. I wonder if Hector's mother knows that despite her son's adorable jack-in-the-box costume he will spend most of the program hidden in the box.

What is it about little girls onstage? My boy child sings a few lines, then hitches up his pants, examines the contents of his nose, and seems a little slack-jawed for the rest of the rehearsal. The girls, in sharp contrast, have real stage presence. Not only do they make eye contact and know all the words to their songs but they sing everyone else's songs and point out to the teacher that Hector is *not* singing in that box. They have to be told several times to stop doing the motions to other people's parts.

I marvel at the talents of the mothers who have made costumes. Who would have guessed that with some spray insulation and Styrofoam teeth a baseball helmet could be turned into a hippopotamus head?

The rehearsal is over by ten-thirty. William invites Ben, another rubber-tree plant, to come home with us. I stop at the grocery store on the way home, and as we walk past the cleaner's, I remember that I've left John's cleaning on the bench in the hall. I never make one trip to this shopping center when two or three in one day are possible. Since I've bought nothing at the store that will melt, I stop at the do-it-yourself car wash on the way home to get some of last night's dust storm off the car. I regret that I'm wearing my only pair of new spring shoes, but the car really does look as if it's been to Lubbock. As I'm racing around the car with the spray wand, one of the rubber-tree plants rolls down his window to ask me a question and I flood the back seat of the station wagon.

Once I've unloaded the groceries, I announce to the boys that we're going to the park for a picnic lunch. I never got the breakfast dishes done, and I can't stand to add to the mess by fixing lunch at home.

It's a gorgeous day in the park. We haven't been here since the summer. Poor William. As third son he has rarely been to the park at all. The scenery has changed a little since my last visit. Today the park is empty except for two young men with their toddler daughters. The men's bicycles are even outfitted with baby seats. From my picnic quilt I observe that these fathers are just as competitive as mothers, comparing notes on how soon their babies walked and how many words they can now say. The men finally grow weary of fetching the curious, staggering pair, who are intent on heading for the creek. They call time out to finish their conversation and plop the tots in the sandpile cylinder. My rubber-tree plants swallow their sandwiches, leave me the crusts, and race off to swing and play pretend games that they seldom get away with in the presence of their older brothers. Drew was probably right when he observed, "Childhood for William just isn't what it used to be." Both boys return thirsty and complain that this isn't much of a picnic since I have only water to offer. I promise that we'll get to school early enough for a frozen yogurt in the cafeteria.

We deposit the picnic basket at home, and I lock Rosie in her pen in the backyard. I expect her to go into heat any day now and worry that the huge Labrador down the street may know it before I do. I slam the gate shut, raking the heads off my husband's onion sets. He refuses to accept that his garden plot is now the dog's pen.

In the school cafeteria the boys get their dessert and I spot the mother of the child who delivered the Girl Scout cookies while we were out of town. We both have trouble figuring the cost of three boxes of cookies at a dollar twenty-five a box. Drew's fourth-grade teacher approaches as I dispatch the rubber trees to their class. "Drew and I have had our wires crossed this week," she tells me, and as if I didn't get the euphemism, she adds, "His attitude is very bad." I assure her that I'm not too fond of his attitude either and encourage her to stay on his case. He has never been highly motivated to do extra work. Only last week he learned the word "mediocre" and now says he thinks it's what he'd like to be.

I stop back at the house, just to be sure the dog is not waltzing with the Lab in her pen. She seems content, so I toss the forgotten cleaning into the car and drive to Sanger Harris to check on an advertised rug sale. I have to park a block away and can't resist stopping in at a sportswear shop to try on bathing suits. I haven't bought a new suit in five years, so it takes courage after perusing the scanty pasties in the front of the shop to ask if anyone still makes a bathing suit with a built-in bra. The saleswoman directs me to some skirted numbers in the back of the store that come no smaller than size 16. I leave without trying anything on.

As I suspected, the rugs in the department store are on sale for good reason. They're ugly. Pulling out of the parking lot, I remember that Jack still needs a chemical for his science project on photosynthesis. If a toy store sells chemistry sets, it follows that it might also sell replacement chemicals. The toy store clerk is certain that the test solution I'm looking for is sodium iodide. I take his word for it, since the section in my brain labeled "Chemistry 601" is vacant except for the word "valence" and a few fond memories of an Australian lab instructor. I am elated to have escaped with this small bottle for a dollar. I was fully prepared to buy a whole chemistry set in desperation.

I remember to take the clothes to the cleaner's this time. As I sort out the bundle on the counter, I notice that it contains the coat to the suit pants I'm picking up.

A new bakery has opened in the shopping strip, so on impulse I buy *pain de campagne* and five chocolate eclairs that will make the frozen pizza we're having for dinner tonight more palatable. At the drugstore I remember to buy poster board. Who can do a science project without poster board? I forget to buy the camera film.

John calls when I get home. He wants to know if I've done three things he wrote down on a "To Do" list for me. I scan the kitchen area near the phone for some scrap of paper he's left me, then confess, "No, I haven't called Texaco to get them to send us a copy of our last two statements, and no, I haven't called the insurance company about the appraisal, and no, I haven't RSVP'd on the invitation to tour the unfinished art museum, but I'll get right on it."

I don't. Instead, I remember to release Jack's geranium

plants from the dark closet where they've been languishing for lack of sunlight in the name of science. Since there won't be two hours of sunlight after Jack gets home from school, I start the project for him by cutting strips of black paper, paper-clipping them to the leaves, and, finally, putting the droopy plants in the sunniest window.

Three-fifteen. Time to meet William at the school crossing. I put the dog on the leash and run the half block for what I call aerobic awareness (it makes me aware that I'm breathless after running half a block). Back home again, William eats a Popsicle while I sort through the huge stack of mail that has dropped through the mail slot. I extract the phone bill and dump the rest in the trash. The two older boys come in the back door at fifteen-minute intervals. I try to monitor the amount they eat while they give me a cursory rundown on their respective days. Drew assures me that he and his teacher have made up. I warn him that he should not go to Todd's house to play Atari, since he has a music lesson at five-thirty and needs to practice. He's not afraid of his music teacher, but I am.

Jack is relieved and genuinely grateful to see my progress on his science project. He rereads his experiment at his desk and yells downstairs, "Do we have any denatured alcohol?" Ooooh, and I thought we could get by with isopropyl. I call the pharmacist, who says, "You know, lady, we get a lot of calls for that, but we don't carry it. Maybe a hardware store would have it." I make a note to stop at the hardware store after I drop Drew off at his music lesson, but first I have to find William's soccer knee pads.

The dog has chewed one knee pad, but when William stuffs it under his long sock it doesn't show. Last week was William's first soccer game against the Blue Mean Machine, and his team won. William never came within twenty feet of the ball, but he now thinks he's some kind of Pelé. "The Gold Stallions are gonna cremate the White Knights," he growls as I drive him to the soccer field. I reintroduce him to his coach, since William says the coach called him Bill last week. I also locate two little friends of his for security and then explain that Mommy has to take Drew to music and Daddy will arrive before the game is over to take him home. He won't buy it. He clings to my skirt and says, "You can't go till Daddy gets here." Fortunately Daddy does arrive. John kisses me right there on the field, even though he knows in his heart that I haven't called Texaco, the insurance company or the museum. "I never saw anybody get kissed on the soccer field," comments the mother of a White Knight.

I dash off to get Drew, who in my absence has, of course, escaped across the alley to play video games at Todd's. I squeal into the driveway, grab the evening paper out of the yard, and honk Drew out of the neighbor's house. Halfway to the music lesson he confesses that he has let the dog out and that he saw her playing with the huge Lab. He promises to call Jack when he gets to his lesson, since I have to get to the hardware store before closing time and the bank clock reads 5:53. The hardware store manager is locking up as I arrive but, seeing the desperate look on my face, he allows me to purchase my denatured alcohol. I pick up some milk at Tom Thumb and still have ten minutes in front of the music teacher's house to scan the *Times Herald*. The musician emerges, and halfway home he admits that he forgot to call Jack about the dog.

As we approach our block, I see a police squad car pulling away. Jack is still shaky from the officer's visit. "He brought Rosie up to the door, and he wanted to talk to you. He said he's gotten complaints about this dog from the neighbors, and Rosie kept making it worse by barking and snarling at him like some mad dog. I thought he was going to arrest me."

John and William return from the soccer game victorious. John takes one look at the desultory frozen pizza and suggests that we all could do with a Mexican-food fix. Jack says he has too much homework but, fearing that he'll eat another Nutty Buddy for dinner if we leave him at home, I insist that he take his spelling homework to the restaurant. Drew dashes upstairs to get some quarters out of his bank in hopes that we'll choose an establishment that has games.

Once we're seated in the restaurant, John forbids anybody to leave the table, then curses the whole video-game industry, which would invade his pleasant family evening of chiles rellenos and beer. While John and I try to review our respective days, the older boys interrupt intermittently to point out what they believe to be homosexuals, transvestites and hermaphrodites dining in this family restaurant. William studies a man with no teeth who is gumming his tostada. I discourage their staring and show them a clipping about their mom that appeared in my hometown paper. I like to remind them from time to time that I have a vocation quite apart from their science projects and dirty socks. "Why do they keep calling you Ms. Mackintosh in this stupid story?" one wants to know. "Do you have multiple sclerosis?"

Home again. Standing up in the kitchen, we eat the lovely chocolate eclairs. I notice that the roaches are letting me down again by coming out when the lights are on. I make a note to call Mr. Thunderbugger.

The small soccer champ is on the verge of hysterical fatigue, so before his older brothers nail him, I dispatch him to the bathtub for a little hydrotherapy. "Read me that book about Bevo, the U.T. Longhorn," he says as I tuck him in for the night.

"We don't have a book about Bevo, do we?" I answer, scanning his bookshelves in search of cowboys, cattle drives or University of Texas football rituals.

"This one," he says, knocking a stack to the floor.

"But this one is about how babies are born."

"It's still got a picture of Bevo on the second page," he insists.

He's right. The drawing of the uterus and ovaries on page 2 does look remarkably like a longhorn. I promise that we'll read this one in the morning.

"Then do the prayer about moon and sun and hills," he says. For a child whose religious education has been thoroughly muddled by his older brothers ("Repent ye and be a convertible"), this son is always comforted by the language of the King James Bible. Or perhaps he's just an adept con man who knows that he can persuade his Southern-Baptist-reared mom to linger at bedtime with a show-off performance of "The sun shall not smite thee by day, nor the moon by night."

Meanwhile, Jack waits in the kitchen to begin the serious laboratory work on the geranium leaves. The denatured alcohol bleaches the leaf nicely, but sodium iodide fails to do its part. Checking my watch, I see regrettably that there is still time for a run to the pharmacy to get some tincture of iodine. Another mother in the drugstore offers her sympathy. Her family has recently purchased an incubator and sacrificed the past three weekends to drive to Pittsburg, Texas, to buy fertilized chicken eggs for a high school science project.

Back in the kitchen, we start the pots boiling again. Rosie has wisely passed out at my feet, and I do feel foolish cooking geranium leaves at nine-thirty. Eureka! Tincture of iodine works. The bleached leaf turns blue, verifying what mankind has probably known since the Enlightenment: plants contain starch. Still we make everyone except sleeping William come downstairs to witness our triumph.

The young scientist is sent to bed, while I examine the yellow iodine stains on my nails and counter tiles. Collapsing in the kitchen rocking chair, I reach for my journal to make sense of a particularly fragmented day. Accomplishments: (1) Jack ate an egg. (2) The dog is not pregnant. (3) The Girl Scout cookies are paid for. (4) The science project —not mine, of course—is completed.

The time-management expert is not amused. What sort of report card is this? Surely there is more. Yes, some musings on the nature of kindergartners, young fathers in the park, and the uneven growth of three sons: the baby who can "cremate the White Knights" but still clings to his mother's skirt, the "mediocre" middle son who currently resists learning that talent without drive is worthless, the firstborn who shows some promising signs of a grateful heart. But what about the writing? The notes scribbled on three-by-five cards during the recounting of dreams, after soccer, and before music lessons will eventually take shape. This sort of life is not without precedent, you know. Harriet Beecher Stowe wrote in this letter to her sister more than a hundred years ago:

> So this same sink lingered in a precarious state for some weeks, and when I had *nothing else to do*, I used to call and do what I could in the way of enlisting the good man's sympathies in its behalf.
>
> How many times I have been in and seated myself in one of the old rocking-chairs, and talked first of the news of the day, the railroad, the last proceedings in

Congress, the probabilities about the millennium, and thus brought the conversation by little and little round to my sink! . . . because, till the sink was done, the pump could not be put up, and we couldn't have any rain-water. Sometimes my courage would quite fail me to introduce the subject, and I would talk of everything else, turn and get out of the shop, and then turn back as if a thought had just struck my mind, and say:—

"Oh, Mr. Titcomb! about that sink?"

"Yes, ma'am, I was thinking about going down street this afternoon to look out stuff for it."

"Yes, sir, if you would be good enough to get it done as soon as possible; we are in a great need of it."

"I think there's no hurry. I believe we are going to have a dry time now, so that you could not catch any water, and you won't need a pump at present."

These negotiations extended from the first of June to the first of July, and at last my sink was completed. . . . Also during this time good Mrs. Mitchell and myself made two sofas, or lounges, a barrel chair, divers bedspreads, pillow cases, pillows, bolsters, mattresses; we painted rooms; we revarnished furniture; we—what *didn't* we do?

Then on came Mr. Stowe; and then came the eighth of July and my little Charley [her seventh child]. I was really glad for an excuse to lie in bed, for I was full tired, I can assure you. Well I was what folks call very comfortable for two weeks, when my nurse had to leave me. . . .

During this time I have employed my leisure hours in making up my engagements with newspaper editors. I have written more than anybody, or I myself, would have thought. I have taught an hour a day in our school, and I have read two hours every evening to the children. The children study English history in school, and I am reading Scott's historic novels in their order . . . ; yet I am constantly pursued and haunted by the idea that I don't do anything. Since I began this note I have been called off at least a dozen times; once for the fishman, to buy codfish; once to see a man who had brought me some barrels of apples; once to see a book-man; then to Mrs. Upham, to see about a drawing I promised to make for her; then to nurse the baby; then into the kitchen to make a chowder for dinner; and now I am at it again, for nothing but deadly determination enables me ever to write; it is rowing against wind and tide. . . .

To tell the truth, dear, I am getting tired; my neck and back ache, and I must come to a close.

Harriet always keeps me from feeling heroic or even modern. Her first installment of *Uncle Tom's Cabin* appeared less than a year after Mr. Titcomb fixed that sink.

Endless Summer

THE REFRIGERATOR door in my kitchen fairly flutters with notices of what's going on during the summer for kids in Dallas. Summer theater programs, vacation Bible schools, art museum classes, tennis camps, computer courses, library story hours, swimming lessons. You name it, I know when and where. I even found a card from a claw-hammer dulcimer instructor while cleaning out my purse yesterday. I gather this information every year with the naive assumption that my sons will be seized by the desire for self-improvement. In the past, William, the worldly wise third son, has attended creative arts classes at Southern Methodist University, where he apparently inspired the class to create only bloodthirsty spiders in a variety of media, but Jack and Drew have traditionally regarded the summer as a time for inertia, interspersed with daily trips to the neighborhood pool. A course in Pac-Man might catch their eye, but any other refrigerator-door offerings will fall to the floor as the yearly scramble for Popsicles inside begins.

Perhaps my childhood summers were really not so different. However, the presence of television and air conditioning almost precludes the comparison. My sons can't know how palpably I longed for summer in late May when the sweat on my arms turned the black ink of my home-work paper greenish. In their seasonless, temperature-controlled classrooms, they've never hoarded wet brown paper towels from the rest room or fought over the posi-tioning of the floor fan, which, in that shimmering heat, seemed only to circulate chalk dust. For us, summer promised a release from confining school clothes and shoes, and the exchange of scheduled boredom for . . . well, unscheduled boredom—days and days of hot noth-ing to do.

Since school never resumed until after Labor Day back then, summers seemed eternal. My family seldom took summer vacations, and no one in those days felt obliged to keep the children entertained—or cool, for that matter.

The relentless, humid East Texas heat was relieved only by an attic fan, which my mother rationed mercilessly. At night she had a sadistic knack, we thought, for snapping off the comforting soporific hum of that fan just at the moment we were drifting off, an act my older brother thought tantamount to unplugging a man's iron lung. (The iron lung image was meaningful, of course, since polio was rampant in Texas in the fifties.) "Just lie still and you'll be cool enough," my mother would call down the hall in response to my brother's exaggerated gasping for air.

While I would not suggest that we do away with the Salk vaccine, I do know that the threat of polio during the fifties afforded my mother and others who subscribed to the two-hour "polio nap" theory of disease prevention a respite during long summer afternoons that mothers of subsequent generations have been denied. My sons have heard about these loathsome naps, the humiliation of having to strip to your underwear after lunch and go to bed in the middle of the day. I think I've told them that I spent those long afternoons reading *Anna Karenina* or listening to radio broadcasts of the Metropolitan Opera. Actually, I read Katy Keene comic books and memorized the words to "How Much Is That Doggie in the Window?"

I suppose television and the ubiquitous video games have rendered obsolete the sort of boredom I knew as a child. Our aimless summer days required some initiative even though ours seldom produced anything more edifying than tying strings to June bugs' legs. We made mud pies in the neighbor's sandpile until somebody objected to our wasting the water from the garden hose. We tried several summers to dig our own swimming pool; and Saturday matinees inspired a few jungle adventures in overgrown honeysuckle caves. When our imaginations failed us, there was always canasta. Aside from required swimming lessons and the naps, adults didn't touch our summer much. There wasn't much going on in my small town; I guess it was just too hot.

Air conditioning makes it possible for a mother like me, oppressed in mid-life by books she never read or the skills she never acquired, to begin the summer with all the resolve of New Year's Day. The need for civilizing influences is obvious as I hear my sons' summer litany: "Wanna bet?" "Oh, bull." "Mom, he touched me again." "Gotcha last!" "I won." "What you say is what you are; you're a 'nekkid' movie star."

My doorbell rings as early as six forty-five in the summer. Some small lisping tot wants to know if William can come out and play. I patiently reestablish the summer receiving hours, and later, still half dressed at seven-thirty, I discover that William has admitted the child through the back door and he's using my bathroom. Only my husband leaves at eight-thirty as usual, and I consider going with him. The older boys sleep until ten. "Perfect timing," Drew says, cocking one eye open. "Just in time for 'The Price Is Right.' Jack Mackintosh, come on down," he yells to Jack in his attic bedroom, in perfect parody of the game-show host. Breakfast seems to last all morning. Cereal bowls and every drinking glass in the cupboard accumulate on the drainboard before noon, when the process begins again. No one seems to be hungry at the same time as anyone else. William and his friend who came at dawn generously distribute to children I've never met all the homemade juice Popsicles I'd intended to last the week. Anarchy is loosed. Neither the front door nor the back door is ever closed, and that valiant heaving air-conditioning compressor in the backyard becomes my kindred spirit.

Last year I had a plan. After their first swim at the neighborhood pool, I interrupted their glut of afternoon cartoons to present each boy with a spiral notebook. "Think of this summer as one long field trip. Don't let it slide by and wonder what you did with it. Set some goals —things you want to learn to do, books you intend to read. You can keep track of it all in these notebooks, and you'll have it made when your teacher in the fall assigns the 'What I Did All Summer' essay. Drew, you and Jack ought to get at least ten books read. Sunday, I thought we'd drive over to Fort Worth to see the Old Masters Collection at the Kimbell. I don't think any of you has ever seen a Rembrandt or a Titian."

The boys regarded me with incredulous stares, as if waiting for the punch line. I unplugged the television, tossed at them the school reading list I'd found buried in somebody's backpack and made a quick exit.

Drew came downstairs about an hour later and announced that, since he'd already finished his ten books, he'd like to plug in the TV for "Fantasy Island."

"What do you mean, you've already read your ten books?"

He tossed his new spiral on the table. "Read 'em and weep, Mom."

There were ten books, all right:

1. *The Hungry Caterpillar*
2. *Curious George Rides a Bike*
3. *Goodnight Moon*
4. *One Fish, Two Fish*
5. *Where the Wild Things Are*
6. *Froggie, Where Are You?* (No words, just pictures. Drew says he read the dedication and the copyright information.)
7. *Happiness Is a Warm Puppy*
8. *Little Bear*
9. *Pat the Bunny*
10. *The Grouchy Ladybug*

"But these are William's books," I protested.

"You didn't say how long they had to be," he shrugged triumphantly. I checked his first journal entry for the day. "Won the book race. Watched 'Fantasy Island.'"

Well, we still had the trip to the Kimbell exhibit on Sunday. To insure a positive attitude about the whole adventure, John and I loaded the car with reviews on the exhibit, Janson's *History of Art for Young People* and something much more elementary, written like a comic book, called *The Usborne Story of Painting*. I also stocked a substantial supply of junk food. There is a direct correlation between my sons' exposure to the finer things of life and the condition of their teeth.

To insure that they would at least look at the paintings, I had read enough about the Old Masters Collection to type out a little treasure hunt for the boys:

Locate the following items in the paintings:

1. a woman in a red dress
2. a knight in armor
3. a small dog
4. a character from a Bible story
5. a ghost
6. a spinning wheel

Rewards for finding the items on the list were their favorite sour apple candies.

When we reached the museum I rented three cassette earphones on the premise that seventeenth-century subjects might be enhanced by a little electronic wizardry. The recorded docent, of course, had far more to say than my little treasure hunters wanted to hear. So eager were they to win the candy I'd promised that they discarded their earphones and raced through the exhibit like the tornado that swept through Paris. Jack, of course, located all the items first and, thinking my treasure hunt was a race, Drew tried to trip him before he could report back to me. By the time I reached them in the last gallery, their bodies were flailing dangerously close to a priceless Palma Vecchio; the museum guard assisted me in expelling them to the courtyard, where I cried and ate their candy.

"I guess we're just not old enough to know how to act in museums," said one of the boys with calculated contrition.

"Face it, Mom," said Jack, "we aren't ever going to like the things you like." William cried all the way home because nobody had shown him the ghost.

When all three boys were tucked in for the night, I pasted three postcards from the Old Masters Collection in each of their journals and wrote, "Saw a Titian. Won the museum race." In my own notebook, I wrote, "A line of Hershey bars from here to Fort Worth wouldn't get my sons to the Kimbell again."

They will go halfway to Fort Worth, however, to Arlington Stadium to watch the Rangers play baseball. One son's first coherent phrase was a perfectly inflected "Col' beah, col' beah" learned at the stadium. Sometimes, on the way to the games, they stage pretend quiz shows for me.

"Mrs. Mackintosh, welcome back to our show. Last week you competed poorly, but we've decided to give you a second chance. If you answer the first question, you may choose to go on to the next category, or you may take the box and go home."

"Take the box, lady, take the box," our imaginary audience yells.

"Well, what is my category this week? Name that aria?" I ask hopefully.

"No, Mrs. Mackintosh, I'm afraid it's SPORTS!" They ask me terrible questions about batting averages, famous base stealers, and World Series trivia that happened before I was born. They delight in my ignorance and introduce me to their friends as the only mother in the world who still says "Brooklyn Dodgers."

Sitting at Arlington Stadium in the left-field bleachers, I enjoy the variety of mankind that gathers for this summer ritual more than the game itself. In that eerie combination of twilight and stadium light, even my own sons look different to me. I am awed by their maleness, the way they take so easily to the heckling and yelling, how quickly they absorb information about men named Cerone and Piniella whom I've never met. I used to know everything in their heads. Who taught them this?

The unsettling jockeying for position that we go

through in June settles into a rather pleasant routine by
July. I have lowered my expectations and have decided
once again that upholding Western civilization is not
solely my responsibility. Jack and Drew by that time are
spending three hours a day at the swimming pool. Their
bodies are golden and their hair is bleached and spiky
from the chlorine. I watch them take off on their bikes
each day with towels tossed jauntily around their necks,
and I wish Norman Rockwell were around to paint them. I
will settle for their learning this year that damp towels left
under the rear seat of the station wagon grow green and
fuzzy and smell almost as bad as the dog vomit we have to
clean up after each trip to the vet.

Never mind that the closest they get to the neighborhood library is the drink machine in the adjoining fire
station, where root beers are still a quarter; they have
pacified me by sitting still on summer evenings for
Kipling's *Jungle Book* or *Tales from the Arabian Nights.* I
know they've listened, since I sometimes hear one call the
other a "queer vizier." We've also read all of D'Aulaire's
Greek Myths, and through the readings aloud we share a
common family mythology that mingles characters from
Dickens with Frank Baum's *Ozma of Oz.* I will be curious
to see who signs up for the summer chore dubbed
"Augean Stables" this year.

Not all of my plans fail. In addition to the random readings on summer evenings, in July my sons usually meet
William Shakespeare as he was perhaps meant to be encountered—outside with plenty of food and drink at the
Fair Park band shell. Jack and Drew were hooked the first
year when I arranged for them to hand out programs for
the Shakespeare Festival of Dallas. Somehow, being a part
of the "staff" with official work to do enhanced the whole
experience. They squirmed and groaned a little when I

read them a quick synopsis from one of their *Shakespeare for Children* books, but, seated on the front row, they were mesmerized by the knife-wielding Shylock and his pound of flesh. *The Taming of the Shrew* that summer was staged in a Wild West saloon. They'll never forget it. I like to think that before they ever meet Shakespeare in a perhaps deadly high school English class they will have seen at least twelve of his plays as sheer entertainment.

Last July, William and I enjoyed a magic garden—a beanstalk, a sensitive plant that recoiled each day from our touch, a sunflower and a tobacco leaf that shriveled first in the Texas heat. Though all our gardening efforts sizzled by midsummer, I am grateful to have one son who shares my pleasure in summer produce. Neither Jack nor Drew, my finicky eaters, will taste a tomato or a Parker County peach. Even John says it's almost obscene the way I eat whole tomatoes as snacks. But William is my heart's delight. He chases pigeons at the Farmers Market, shells "cream peas" with me on the porch and exclaims over the crispness of 'cumbers. "My eyes taste it to my tummy!" he says, sniffing whatever I'm cooking. If I ever win a vacation to the South of France, I'm buying him a ticket.

In August there are sometimes glimmers of ingenuity to applaud. Oh, nobody announces, "Won't my music teacher be surprised if I learn this new piece before September?" And nobody asks me to help with the typing of a clever newsletter for our street. No, an unexpected summer storm one year dropped a huge limb from the dying hackberry in our front yard. Instead of hauling it to the parkway as their dad suggested, all the neighborhood children gathered to nest in it. By noon it had a HOME SWEET HOME sign and three aluminum lawn chairs propped precariously in it. Beach towels draped over limbs provided cozy tent areas, and someone pilfered several extension cords so they could install my toaster and two buzz fans in this tree house on the ground. Well, it certainly beat painting the porch with water again, which was what I was about to suggest.

By August the neighborhood pool has begun to lose its appeal. I always look enviously at the women who are on the last pages of their fourth 500-page novel. At the beginning of summer I had counted twenty-six books piled beside my bed that I could hardly wait to read. My stack has been diminished by one book in August—the tiny Cheever novel. Although my last baby is now a swimmer, I still have to be on the lookout for what John Irving in *The World According to Garp* called "the Undertoad." I am the eternal spectator to every "Watch this, Mom." "Mom, you weren't watching. . . ."

Sometimes in August I do this watching at the beach in Port Aransas. "Watch me carefully now, Mom," one of them cautions as he wades out into the waves. "I wouldn't want to go to a watery grave." What has he been reading?

When the summer ended, I couldn't resist checking my boys' largely undisturbed journals. There were lots of blank pages, a few tic-tac-toe games, poker scores, ubiquitous laser ships shooting each other, "Shutup dumby Drew," and finally an entry made in August at the beach: "The ocean is just like the 7-Eleven; it never closes."

It's not exactly Keats, but it sure beats "Gotcha last."

10 *Downhill All the Way*

A SKIING trip to Vail, Colorado, had never been one of my vacation fantasies. A rustic mountain cabin with a broad front porch, rocking chairs, a clear stream, and a heart-stopping view of aspen-covered slopes, perhaps, but I never had any desire to ski. The truth is, that year I was outvoted. The boys were then aged ten, eight and four and did not long to leave their hearts in San Francisco, the South of France, or the British Museum any more than their mother longed to risk life and limb on icy mountain slopes.

The prospect of such an adventure was considerably enhanced, however, by the fact that we'd be going with our good friends Sue and Walter and their children. They were seasoned skiers and could minimize our mistakes in packing and planning. I also had the absurd illusion that we'd save some money on this trip by sharing a house and doing all our own cooking. We even got some bargain ski gear. Walter happened on a going-out-of-business ski warehouse sale and outfitted my older boys with skis, poles, boots, and bindings—the works—for less than we could rent them in Colorado. Jack and Drew were so excited about the trip that frequently I returned home from running errands to find that they had dragged their discount gear down from the attic and cross-countried my bedroom floor. Telltale pole punctures remain in the Kool-Aid-stained carpet even now. I bought as little equipment as possible for myself and borrowed clothes from a family of daughters for four-year-old William, warning Jack and Drew that I'd shred their lift tickets if they made one crack about the rosebuds on Willie's thermal underwear.

Jack and his dad had been skiing once before, and while John tried to allay my fears Jack tormented his archrival younger brother with his experience. "How are you gonna stop your skis when you're about to crash into somebody, Drew? . . . You know what happens if you don't lift your skis at the end of the lift? Your legs get ripped off." I tried not to think about the lift.

John kept reassuring me. "If you don't like it, you can just stay in the house and read by the fire. You don't have to ski." He knew, of course, that my puritan conscience could never justify paying exorbitant rent for a house in Vail just to read a trash novel by the fire. No, I'd have to ski.

Some friends who grew up in Dallas have an affinity for Colorado that predates the pervasive condo-in-the-Rockies syndrome. Back in the early fifties, many of them were sent to breathe Colorado's purer air every summer to avoid polio. They lived in rather inaccessible rustic cabins with wood-burning stoves and acquired some enviable wilderness skills. I looked forward to seeing the mountains they'd told me about. Such grandeur would, I thought, diminish the arrogance that comes from living in a place where the best of the scenic beauty, the azaleas along Turtle Creek in April, is just further evidence of man's accomplishments.

I probably went to the wrong place. Vail was built in part with Dallas money. The mountains are spectacular, of course, but they seem so tame when harnessed with lifts and gondolas and perfectly manicured and well-marked slopes. As for the town, I had fully expected Vail to be as fake Tyrolean as the European Crossroads shopping center in Dallas. It wasn't. It was tasteful and clean and efficient. But in a way I felt as if I'd stumbled onto a village in the Twilight Zone. The people on the streets looked like aliens or astronauts in an experimental space station, all of them uniformed in ski clothes like those I'd borrowed. Tomorrow, I thought, I'd look like one of them in my navy nylon bib overalls, crayon-colored turtleneck, pom-pommed hat, and goggles. The parking attendants, store clerks, waiters, and ski instructors seemed to be clones—not because they all looked alike, though many of them did, but because they all performed their duties with such remarkable patience, cheerfulness, and courtesy.

All we accomplished that first day was grocery shopping, unpacking in the spacious but singularly unremarkable house, and renting ski equipment for John, William, and me. I hadn't allowed myself to look carefully at molded plastic ski boots before. Once my flat foot and thick calf were bolted into that heavy shoe, I knew it was going to be hard to fake having a good time.

The next day, loading the van with boots, poles, skis, caps, and mittens for ten people, registering children in their respective ski classes and securing lift tickets made me long for the lazy vacations we've enjoyed at Port Aransas. Hassle on those trips meant shaking sand out of my novel and deciding who had to carry the inner tubes. To compound the morning's difficulties, William did not take to Small World, the much-praised kindergarten near the ski area, the way my friends had assured me he would. The walls of the little schoolhouse were lined with pictures of smiling tots on tiny skis. Two more cheerful, capable clones, Sandy and Debbie, efficiently labeled William and his tiny gear with masking tape and pried him loose from my Hollofil nylon thighs, assuring me that he'd be skiing Gopher Hill by afternoon. I limped to my ski class with his plaintive cries still ringing in my ears.

How could this be a vacation? It was only ten o'clock and I was exhausted. Waiting for the ski instructor to appear, I tried to size up my classmates. Who were these people inside the multicolored down jackets? We chatted nervously with each other, anticipating our failures, trying desperately to establish some worthy identity apart from our garish hats and the pitiable strength of our ankles. One woman I pegged correctly as a show-off, the sort who joins exercise classes to display her excellent body in a leotard. She would feign ignorance at first, then astound the handsome young instructor with her graceful parallel form. A rotund middle-aged New Yorker, sweating profusely just from carrying his skis and poles up the gentle slope known as the Golf Course, kept grousing to his snow bunny girl friend, "I tol' ya we shoulda gone to Vegas." Mickey, a dental hygienist from Omaha, was there with her boyfriend Dan, who though muscular and outdoorsy-looking proved to be the most inept skier in our class. Not only did he fall each time he descended the little practice hill but he was never able to right himself again without Mickey's assistance. If their relationship weathered this ski trip, I thought, their marriage prospects were excellent.

Other classmates included four women about my age from South Carolina. With everyone's face half obscured by goggles, the inveterate people watcher in me had to be satisfied with dialect distinctions. Those warm South Carolina voices comforted me in ways the slightly nasal Nebraska or Minnesota ones never could. "Hi, ah'm Betty, and this is Patty and Ann and Addie. Weah heah with owa doctah husbands who ah much bettah skiuhs." Somehow I doubted that women who routinely passed the time of day at such a languid tempo would be in any hurry to hurl themselves recklessly down icy slopes. Betty, I noticed, never even wore her ski cap. "Messes up yuh haiuh, yuh know."

Bob, our ski instructor, was a twenty-three-year-old blond Nordic prince from Minnesota. He had taught skiing for twelve years, he said, competed successfully in Austrian competition, and given private instruction to the likes of Dustin Hoffman and Robert Redford only the week before. Although his encouraging and patient demeanor never faltered, I felt certain that he retreated to the instructors' lounge every afternoon and beat his head against the wall. Bob taught us to wedge, or snowplow, our way down gentle slopes. I would have been content with that achievement for the week, had the pain of sidestepping back up the hill in skis been adequately compensated for by the thrill of the descent. My boots rubbed bruises on my lower shins and blisters on my ankles, so that eventually I longed to graduate to the ski lift just to be able to sit down for a few minutes. Betty, however, was afflicted with acrophobia, which in this clime meant a nauseating fear of ski lifts.

I have no abnormal fear of heights; my phobia is machinery or, for that matter, any life experience involving conveyor belts or moving parts that proceed without regard for the probability of human error. It's an uneasiness that I recall from childhood, when I feared the sting of the jump rope on my legs if I miscalculated my entry. In adult life, of course, it is the anxiety of entering Central Expressway from the access road.

The instructions for the ski lift were unsettling: STAND ON THE BLUE LINE. LET ONE CHAIR GO BY, THEN MOVE QUICKLY TO THE RED LINE. PLACE YOUR SKI POLES IN YOUR INSIDE HAND AND LOOK OVER YOUR SHOULDER TO SEE THE APPROACHING CHAIR. I didn't like that word "quickly." Sometimes I could move my skis quickly and sometimes I couldn't. Sometimes they just sort of slid sideways on the ice and made no forward progress at all. With Bob's assistance I caught the right chair on the lift and then was faced with the frightening signs posted along the way: CHECK FOR LOOSE CLOTHING. Had I zipped the dozen or so zippers on my Day-Glo parka? How could I check? I had ski poles clutched tightly in one hand and the other hand white-knuckled to the armrest of the chair. PREPARE TO UNLOAD. LIFT SKIS. No matter how badly my shins ached, I got those skis up.

The second time I rode the lift, a little girl in front of me did not get her skis up, and I watched her leg twist at an ugly angle. The ski safety patrol was there in a matter of seconds, strapping her to a stretcher sled and whisking her away so fast that I doubt the chair behind me even knew there had been an accident. Although I was grateful for their swift response, I also wondered cynically if they were just part of a conspiracy to maintain the illusion that this was a hazard-free sport. Were they constantly sweeping the mountain clean of fallen bodies so the rest of us would come back next year?

Our ski instructor, who said that he also biked ten miles a day to stay in shape, had no concept of the stamina levels he had been assigned in this class. Most of the women, including me, admitted to being winded after the morning sprint upstairs to see if the children were indeed out of bed. We begged for coffee breaks, and two even ignored his reproving stares and had a furtive smoke or two on the slopes. At one point my mouth was so dry—probably from hyperventilating down the last slope—that when I wiped out (the only way I knew how to stop that first day) I grabbed a handful of snow and ate it. "Spit that out," Bob yelled. "It's not real snow. These beginner slopes are blown every morning with a petroleum-based artificial snow." More of God's Colorado grandeur. I ate the snow anyway.

Lunch provided another chance to sit down and un-buckle the painful boots. Deliberately oblivious to our instructor's impatience, we prolonged the noon repast with that effortless and sometimes grotesque conversation that flows from Southern women—stories of straying husbands and untimely hysterectomies, hilarious sketches of sons "taken drunk" at Clemson. Layers of clothing granted us further excuse for delays in the ladies' room after lunch.

Finally back on the slopes in the afternoon, Bob praised us as we gradually learned to stop without falling. Now he began to chip away at our self-imposed caution. "Let her rip, Priscilla," Bob yelled at me as I continued to wedge to slow my skis on an icy traverse. As the inclines grew steeper, slowing up required more strength than I pos-sessed and Bob mistook my speed for gay abandon. When the lesson was over I reminded him that my name was Prudence, not Priscilla, and suggested that he might do well to look it up in his dictionary.

At three-thirty every afternoon the lifts closed. I have heard friends who purport to love this sport confess that the best time of the day is getting to the base of the mountain and knowing that you don't have to go up again.

As I staggered toward the lodge in my torturous boots, I tried to carry my skis jauntily locked together over one shoulder. The bindings, however, bruised my collarbone, so I just dragged them the last twenty yards. While I waited for my family I overheard men comparing their times down certain slopes and talking of maneuvering tricky moguls (snow-covered obstacles on more difficult slopes) or of having skis rewaxed for more speed. Skiing, I suppose, allows hard-driving men and women, the sort who run marathons for fun and who can't really relax on vacations, ample opportunity to continue competing and pushing themselves while technically satisfying their doctors' orders that they take a few days off. I was not surprised to read in that afternoon's paper that a middle-aged man from Houston had suffered a fatal heart attack on the slopes. I had certainly undergone more stress in the past five hours on that mountain than I ever encountered in my hectic daily routine. How had this sport become so popular? Was everyone afraid to admit that the emperor wore no clothes? Was I the only adult who felt a little embarrassed at having paid eighteen dollars to slide painfully down a mountain?

Reunited with my family, I found that only little William seemed to be his mother's child. At Small World, he had steadfastly refused to leave the security of his rest mat all day, despite the cheerful coaxing of Debbie and Sandy. John, relying on his one-time-only experience, had bravely skied the whole day with Walter and Sue. He acknowledged his need for ski school the second day. My older sons were thoroughly exhilarated, and I saw the virtue of our being apart all day. Separate ski classes had allowed each of us the freedom to gloss over our first-day failures. Unseen on the lift above, I had glimpsed Drew falling and crying in the snow. But his pell-mell report made no mention of tears or frustration—only speedy descents of Gopher Hill. "Kathy, my teacher—Mom, you'd like her a lot, she's all over her zits, she's twenty-one and has six brothers and she used to live on a farm—well, she thought my skis were too big for me, but I did okay with 'em. The kid in front of me on the lift barfed every time we got off." Disdaining all beginner slopes, Jack had kept up with far more experienced skiers all day long. "Jack needs to practice his parallel turns more," his teacher told me. "He goes straight down the hills." I knew that he had been too embarrassed to tell her that he didn't know how to make parallel turns, and he had simply skied straight down slopes at breakneck pace with his heart in his throat all day.

When we got back to the house my experienced skiing friends revealed a complete inventory of Dr. Scholl's assorted foot remedies. As I looked gratefully at the Dopp Kit full of doughnut sponges, corn pads and moleskin, it hit me that Sue and Walter had anticipated and accepted this pain much the way we accept the probability of diarrhea in Mexico. The ten of us were in our beds by nine-thirty. John had assured me that the sleep after a day of skiing was the deepest, best sleep I'd ever experience. He was wrong. I skied all night. Each time I closed my eyes the white ground sheeted beneath me at terrifying speeds.

The next morning, well padded with Band-Aids and moleskin, we went our separate ways. I fell down less in my class that day but agreed with my South Carolina friend Betty that there was a speed beyond which we had no desire to go. She and I decided that we would take off our skis and walk if the slopes we encountered appeared to exceed our internal speed limits.

Although I knew that my stamina and ability would

never match my sons' or husband's, I made one valiant
attempt to ski with them later in the week at Beaver
Creek, a newer ski area near Vail. To say I performed
poorly that day is an understatement. I fell four times in
less than ten minutes. I cried in front of my children, and
although they were solicitous at first, they finally abandoned me in disgust. We met up again on the Grand
Traverse, a flat but icy roadway that led to the mid-moun-
tain restaurant. My boys cheered me wildly as I skied
along at their pace. I was glad that my goggles kept them
from seeing the look of horror in my eyes.

"You know," John said on the airplane going home,
"you weren't half bad up there. Once you got going, you
did just fine. You'll be a lot better next year."

"Next year?"

11 Bees and Birds

"HAVE YOU seen a prostitute?" Drew's friend from San Antonio asked him as I drove the two of them home from the airport.

"No," Drew replied without much interest, "I don't think it's been to Dallas yet."

My kid's not slow. He just lacks the proper vocabulary. Now, if Travis had said "hooker," some serious discussion might have ensued.

When this child was four, he withdrew his life savings ($3.30) from his piggy bank and headed down the alley where an enterprising neighbor's child was vending his father's discarded girlie magazines. Moments later Drew returned, thoroughly pleased at having invested the whole sum in an anniversary issue of *Playboy*.

He didn't try to hide it from me. In fact, since it was his nap time, he suggested that we peruse his treasure on my bed where we'd heretofore read Oz books and Pooh poems. Why not? Even Mister Rogers himself sang, "Every body's fancy, every body's fine. Your body's fancy and so is mine."

I hadn't seen a *Playboy* in years. In that interim there had clearly been a shift in the photographers' focus from bountiful bosoms to nether regions. As we turned past the initial after-shave ads and cartoons, I began to regret that the kid hadn't had the sense to stash this under his mattress.

"Uh, Drew," I stammered, "well, what do you think about these ladies . . . uh, girls?" I prayed that he was focusing, as I tried to, on the vacuity of their expressions. "I mean, do these look like girls you'd like to have as playmates, uh, friends? Do you think they'd be fun to talk to?"

"Sure, Mom," he said, pointing to a page displaying Misses January through December. "They all look just like you, except they do their hair different."

In retrospect, I was obviously conned by a four-year-old who knew I couldn't fly into a fit over a book full of mommies. When I related the misdemeanor to John, he confiscated the evidence and disappeared for the evening.

Playboy has never replaced *The Jungle Book* for naptime reading, but clearly our children are more worldly wise than we were at their age. The fifties, of course, was not an era of sexual explicitness. What sex information we gleaned in our elementary school days may have been furtively procured, but by today's standards it was remarkably innocent. One friend and I sometimes got down her father's heavy medical books. Looking at diseased parts, we concluded, was better than nothing. My husband must have been more adventurous. While trying to interest his sons in the pleasures of stamp collecting, he recently came across a "feelthy picture" he had secreted away with his Mozambique triangles at age eleven. "I bought that at the bowling alley where I set pins—cost me a day's pay, I remember," he said. "It was a little disappointing even then," he admitted as the boys and I convulsed over this black and white photograph of a nude, overweight Hispanic woman making an obscene gesture.

Grace Metalious' *Peyton Place* was as steamy a tome as we passed from locker to locker in high school. Other bits of information and misinformation were pieced together from jokes, friends, older brothers, John O'Hara paperbacks carelessly discarded by adults, and a Kimberly-Clark publication called *Very Personally Yours* which I was sure had been left in my room by mistake. Movies fed our romantic impulses but left everything to our imaginations with quick fades and mysterious gestures. While I don't remember any grim lectures from my parents, it was an uncomplicated time to be a female teenager. The only rule to remember was DON'T. And most of us didn't. A friend returning to his twentieth-year high school reunion took an informal survey of his successful male classmates several weeks in advance. Pretending to need their advice on business, he closed their office doors and presented them with a list of all the girls in the class. "Just check off the ones you scored with in high school." One after another, they scanned the list and sheepishly slid it back across the desk unmarked. At the reunion my friend concluded that the men of the class had either become senile, discreet, or just honest enough to admit that most high school conquests were feats of imagination.

Despite our rather innocent childhoods, as parents we have imbued our own offspring with accurate and explicit anatomical terms before they've learned to lisp their last names. On a car trip to visit my parents, Drew once asked his father to repeat the whole clinical outline of the sperm's heroic journey to the ovum. Jack, by that time, was old enough to be so mortified by Drew's request that he hid on the floorboards. I wanted to join him, since John kept saying "the mommy and the daddy" instead of male and female. When John had completed the lecture, easier this time with his eyes riveted on the road, Drew responded, "Yuk! Don't anybody hand me another cheese cracker or talk about stopping for a hamburger. I think I'm gonna throw up."

Our children can't fathom how daring it seems for us to say these words we never even heard our own parents whisper. Such candor, of course, does bring embarrassing moments. The other day I watched with great sympathy a young mother with her daughter in the grocery store checkout line. The daughter, about three years old, was busy sorting out the various people in the store according to gender. Pointing to Winnie, the checker, the child said, "Winnie got a 'gina. Mama got a 'gina, and you," she said, pointing to the hulking construction worker standing just behind her mother, "have a penis, don't you?" Johnny Carson himself could not have launched into a quicker ad-lib conversation than that poor mother. "Oh," she said, reading the man's company shirt pocket, "I see you work for HCB Company. I've seen some of their buildings. They look very sturdy. I'll bet you have to do some very dangerous work climbing out on those steel girders—or maybe you drive one of these big tall cranes—Ceci, he works like Mike Mulligan and his steam shovel. . . ."

I myself have blanched in the drugstore when one of mine yells across three aisles with total nonchalance, "Mom, don't forget to get something for that mosquito bite on my scrotum."

Perhaps we were hasty in discarding the wonderful euphemisms of our own childhoods. Certainly we have deprived our children of a rich heritage of language that could eliminate some of this embarrassment in public places. I had a great-aunt who, either from living through droughts or perhaps with outdoor plumbing, never believed in long luxurious baths. She felt that a sponge bath done properly was perfectly adequate and used to dispatch me to the bathroom with the instructions: "Just wash as far as possible . . . and then wash possible." And then there was Granny Paup, my friend's grandmother who, when referring to male private parts (and believe me, it wasn't often), used the term "his fatal thing." While I wouldn't wish my children to be limited to Victorian "possibles" and "fatal things," a few hilarious alternatives to grim anatomical terminology are surely in order. As one friend says, "Sex is fun and funny. What more can you say?"

At fourteen, twelve and even seven there is scarcely any cold fact about sex that these boys haven't heard. A first grader can and does sound out the word "rape" in the headlines. The recent glut of newspaper and television reports on child abuse and controversy over abortion have left no ugly aspect of life unexamined. At school my boys are cautioned about child molesters. At their friends' houses I have no doubt they have watched movies on cable channels that would scar me for life. John, as a trial lawyer, frequently discusses malpractice cases in great gynecological detail at the dinner table. When we leave our favorite Mexican food restaurant, my sons quickly abandon their father to walk hand in hand with me because they are well aware that we are in a predominantly gay neighborhood.

We seem to spend a disproportionate amount of time discussing aberrant sexual behavior with our children. The world intrudes with more candor than we intended.

The important things we want them to know can never be communicated quite so directly. Like all conscientious American parents, we have bought them books on the subject. I bought *Where Did I Come From?* and *What's*

Happening to Me? primarily because the cartoon drawings presume that a sense of humor is essential to any
discussion of sex. However, the printed page inevitably
treats sex as an abstraction, something separate from the
rest of life. Biology class at school may suggest that it's just
another bodily function like sneezing. The phrase "having sex" always sounds to me like "having chicken pox" or
worse, like having a standardized Big Mac in a Styrofoam
container. We don't want our sons to view sex as fast food,
as something that has no bearing on life except for the
moment of gratification. Separating sex from social and
ethical considerations trivializes life itself. As George
Leonard wrote in his book *The End of Sex,* "Such thinking
ignores the fact that we're dealing with a powerful urge
that can enhance a lifelong relationship, transform a human body and even lead to the creation of life."

But where do kids bombarded with TV titillation and
the instant thrill of video games pick up on the subtleties
and mysteries that can't be pictured in textbooks?

I hope it's communicated as wordlessly at our house as it
was in the home where I grew up. Somehow, without
worrying about it the way we do, my parents managed to
communicate the broader implications of sexuality that
have to do with a man and a woman loving each other so
much that even after fifty years together they still sometimes dance in the kitchen. They created a hugging, kiss-
ing, laughing and sentimental crying family. But aside
from these obvious gestures, when my parents are together there is an implicit sense of intimacy that has to do
with eyes and hands and hearts.

As a child I knew their bed as a source of comfort to my
brother and me. It was also a place of hilarity, a place for
giggling with the lights out or for talking about the things

you couldn't say face to face. Their bed was a good place to be.

I think I've passed that on. I've given up on the linen pillow shams that could make our bed with its ornate Victorian headboard look like the ones in magazines. Our bed is usually a mess. The boys' tag team matches often begin there as they jockey for position to hear a favorite story. Sometimes we do hard algebra problems there and on a cold morning John and I may snuggle a boy or two.

No child, I'm convinced, wants to think about his parents having intercourse, much less have a conversation with them about it. Some things are better learned by osmosis. In my parents' house, I learned a lot about giving and receiving affection. I learned that a rich and intimate relationship thrives on patience, trust, forgiveness, humility and laughter. If *that*, absurd as it must always seem to a young child, was also a part of it, then so be it. Their experience was uniquely their own and mine would be another variation because love is not a standardized commodity.

Dr. Jerry Lewis, director of research and training at Timberlawn Psychiatric Institute in Dallas, has been shocking audiences for many years in his talks on healthy families. He says, "I'm in favor of as much sexual education for children as possible. Certainly the home is the best place—and to be more specific," he says as the thunderous applause dies down, "in the kitchen." There is always a collective gasp while he pursues the theme that, in addition to learning about the heroic journey of the sperm searching for the ovum, there is the even more important business of learning what it is like to be male and to be female. Important lessons in this are frequently held in the kitchen. Children observe the way husbands and wives greet each other in the morning and at the end of the day. Do they kiss? Does it look like fun? Or is it perfunctory? Do they touch? Hug? Are they sensitive to each other's fatigue? Basically, it's just one place where children learn a lot about human beings giving and receiving affection.

The kitchen is also where I learn William's latest riddles:

> "Knock, knock."
> "Who's there?"
> "Egor."
> "Egor who?"
> "Egor for your body."
> "Know what rhymes with China?"

You don't want to know.

12 *The Way to a Woman's Heart*

AS THE representative of all things female in this household, I am often expected to explain or interpret the behavior of my gender. It isn't easy. I have settled disputes about why women wear panty hose. Surveying my corns and bunions, William maintains, "It's to hide their 'gross' feet." I have also had to explain why girls cry so much and why Eugenia thinks you love her when all you did was borrow her paintbrush in art class.

Social change and feminist politics call much of my proffered wisdom into question. (I still think girls shouldn't call.) However, I offer my sons one bit of timeless advice with absolute confidence: "Learn to dance. Women love it."

I have talked with several women my age, each of whom admits that her husband's dancing ability weighed heavily in his favor when she considered his marriage proposal. "I thought that if everything else in our lives became as boring as Velveeta cheese we could still go dancing," one said. Another said, "I wanted the man I married to have three things: a job, a car and the ability to dance. I compromised on the third, but I keep hoping that he'll learn to like it." A wiser woman admitted that she made it part of a prenuptial agreement. "I was his second wife, and I was agreeing to raise his teenage children, so I felt I could extract one promise: there would be dancing —whole evenings of dancing."

I have heard women of all ages recall some spectacular dancer in their lives. They can remember what they wore and the music the band played, but they treasure most the memory of themselves: "I felt like a feather or a butterfly floating in his arms." They also never forget the times they did not dance. "Whenever I meet a man my age who went to Camp Stewart the same summers I went to Camp Mystic thirty years ago, I want to kick him in the shins," said one friend. "Every year for six years I dutifully packed my semiformal, and in all those summers no one ever asked me to dance." Women who grew to a height of five-nine or taller in junior high never quite got over their feelings of uneasiness before dances. "Even at thirty-four, I still worry about what sort of shoes will make me short enough to dance with the best dancers," says one woman of fashion-model proportions. Dancing with a man who's six-four is apparently every tall woman's dream. "You just don't know how rarely we get to lean against a man's chest," one sighed.

Perhaps our love of dancing is part of a deeply rooted desire to be dependent. But that's not the only reason women love to dance. Many women have a lot of rhythm pulsing through their bones, and a good bit of exhibition-ism as well. Women also tend to be looser jointed and less inhibited than men. I remember seeing an Off-Broadway play called *A Coupla White Chicks Sitting Around Talking.* In the first scene, a Westchester housewife in a crisp apron polishes her kitchen and irons her husband's Jockey shorts. Gradually, however, the rock music on her kitchen radio overtakes her, and she throws herself with total abandon into a Tina Turner routine. The nervous laughter of women in the audience told me that they, too, had danced their secret fantasies at home alone. Aerobic dancing and Jazzercise, I'm convinced, are popular for more than the health benefits. Women just don't have enough dancing in their lives.

It has been my good fortune never to be without a dancing partner. My father danced with me before I could walk, and on occasion we are still seen gliding cheek to cheek in my parents' kitchen. Songs like "It Had to Be You" evoke genuine nostalgia for me. I have danced a whole generation longer than most of my contemporaries and done the steps that now seem to be the province of late movies. One cannot just glide around to "How could Red Riding Hood/Have been so very good/And still kept the wolf from the door?" It's a syncopated bounce step, a certain movement in the shoulders, a certain magic in my seventy-seven-year-old partner.

Reminiscing about his college days as Buffalo (as in "Shuffle Off to . . .") Mahaffey, my daddy recently wrote to me, "While I took no prizes in college algebra, no one could say that I was not the best dancer at Furman University. When Amaryllis Pride and Buffalo suddenly burst forth into a wild version of the Charleston, the other dancers momentarily suspended their two-stepping to watch and to wonder." He now confesses that he spent most of his college days learning new dance steps like the Chicago Johnny and the toddle, from the black janitor at his dormitory. He also admits that he once cashed a personal check for two hundred and fifty dollars to help book Ted Weems and His Orchestra into a local hotel. "My father must have known I was not Phi Beta Kappa bound when he saw 'for books' written at the bottom of that check." Plenty of women who have danced with Daddy in the past fifty years would say it was money and time well spent.

While I was never as light on my feet as Amaryllis Pride, I grew up believing that I was a good dancer. So dancing with my eleven-year-old contemporaries in dance class at the Spring Lake Park Pavilion came as something of a shock. Doing the jerky slow-slow-quick-quick-slow with reluctant, sweaty-palmed boys made me realize that I was only as smooth as my partner. My daddy was a hard act to follow. Gradually, of course, my classmates and I learned to slide around a little in time to the music—though it scarcely required any rhythmic sense. This was the era of the strapless Nadine formal. The fluffy nylon net bodices of those dresses were so stiffly constructed with stays that they could have gone to the dances without us. My greatest fear was not so much that I might not keep the strapless dress up but that in reaching up to dance with some basketball player I might leave the heart-shaped construction hugging my waist and reveal just how little the shapely dress and I had in common. While my body did not assume the proportions I longed for in those gruesomely self-conscious seventh- and eighth-grade years, at least it had the good sense to remain below five feet until the shrimpy boys my age began growing in the ninth grade.

Rock 'n' roll music, which in my hometown debuted with "Hearts made of stone . . . doo-de-wah, doo-de-wah," materialized just in time for our first dances. In retrospect, it destroyed a lot of the romanticism that had lingered on dance floors since World War II. We still learned to jitterbug to "Tuxedo Junction" and "Mack the Knife" like our older brothers and sisters, but more and more of our dancing energies were expended on dancing at arm's length from our partners—doing the bop, the hully-gully, the stroll, the mashed potato, and, by the time we were seniors in high school, the twist. These were mainly head-jerking, pelvis-pumping dances that had been done before, but not by our immediate forebears.

Those wildly uninhibited dances drove away a lot of boys who might otherwise have grown up dancing. The girls got to practice at slumber parties and perfected their routines in front of mirrors in the ladies' rest room when the band took a break. The boys, on the other hand, had no comparable testing ground and no reassurance that their loping and gyrating looked anything but foolish.

We still did some slow dancing to endless repetitions of "Silhouettes," "Come Softly to Me," or "Theme from *A Summer Place,*" but our fox-trots and waltzes lacked the ritual sophistication that my father's generation had known. Dance cards and stag lines were a thing of the past. "Who cut in?" my father would always ask when I returned from a school dance. "No one, Daddy." I'd shrug. "I went with Tommy." I'm sure he concluded that I was hopelessly unpopular. What I didn't tell him was that Tommy and I danced so close to each other that my carnation was smashed flat at the end of the evening. A taller friend recalls that her corsage always smelled of hair oil. Dancing so entwined with a number of boys would have seemed downright risqué to my father—a far cry from his day, when he surreptitiously copped a little squeeze during that pause in "In the Mood."

Because my father's family was Methodist he never suffered any of the pangs of conscience about dancing that those of us who were born-again Baptists did. No one seemed concerned that our Baptist Training Union hayrides were nothing short of necking parties; what clearly placed us in Satan's grip was missing prayer meeting on Wednesday night to attend a dance at the Knights of Columbus hall. While God might have smiled on King David's "cutting the fool" before the Ark of the Covenant, we suspected that most of our dancing, like Salome's, was evil. Didn't the Arthur Murray instructor himself say, "No woman can waltz virtuously and waltz well"?

When a silver-tongued, crippled evangelist, perhaps embittered by the physical infirmity that denied him the pleasures of dancing, came to my church and inveighed against the lust incited in teenagers by dancing and "mixed bathing" (boys and girls swimming together), I was among the first down the aisle to sign his pledge cards. In my thirteenth year I forswore dancing, drinking and card playing and signed on for a lifetime of service to the heathen in the Congo, where the seductive strains of Johnny Mathis' "The Twelfth of Never" could not reach me. The Church's prohibition of dancing, of course, made it all the more desirable. With considerable guilt, I reneged on my dancing pledge in time for the Y-teen Valentine dance.

By the time I reached college, dancing was in a serious decline. The North Texas or West Texas push, a dance that still required a partner, barely withstood the onslaughts of the frug and the Watusi. I was awfully glad my father wasn't around to see the alligator—horizontal writhing on beer-sloshed floors to the primal scream of "Shout!" The kids who followed us in the late sixties and early seventies seemed to have renounced dancing altogether for protest marches and chemically induced enchantment.

It's hard for me to fathom courtship without dancing. Like many couples, John and I met at a wedding. He abandoned his designated bridesmaid to escort me from the church to the reception, where we danced into the wee hours. I never hear "Fly Me to the Moon" without remembering that night. After we were engaged, we made an official inspection trip to Brownsville to seek the approval of his eighty-year-old grandmother. Although she thought my ankles could have been thinner, she heartily approved of my long neck, and we celebrated Granny's blessing by dancing at the legendary Drive-In night club across the Rio Grande in Matamoros. I don't know whether it's nostalgia for that evening or just the irresistible romantic quality of Latin music that still makes us dance whenever we listen to our battered copy of Trio Los Panchos singing schmaltzy numbers like "Nuestro Amor" or "Sin Ti."

Perhaps because I grew up dancing, it has never struck me as peculiar that John and I sometimes dance in the kitchen to the radio. While he did launch a rather spectacular campaign to win my hand in 1965, my husband is not the sentimental sort who sends flowers or unexpected gifts. We just like to dance, and certain tunes require it. We've even picked up a few new steps through the years. In 1978, John Travolta and *Saturday Night Fever* prodded thousands of people onto the dance floor. We never made it to a real disco, though we talked about it a lot, but one friend whose husband dances only under duress surprised us with a gift of group disco lessons. We gathered in a mirrored studio—five women in strappy high heels and five weary, gray-flanneled husbands in heavy wing tips. Buddy, our liquid-hipped black instructor, made our men look like a chorus line of Tin Woodmen. We never got much beyond basic hustle steps, but afterward, over beer at the Pizza Inn, we agreed the lessons had been fun. I thought of reconvening the group the next year for a tango project.

As my contemporaries turn forty, fewer and fewer men are dancing at all. Social functions organized by women inevitably include dancing, but the men seem to regard parties as opportunities to conduct business. The division of the sexes at dances is almost as bad as it was when we were twelve. There are plenty of reasons men don't dance. Some never learned. "I know I'd be a better husband if I could dance," said one repentant soul, "but I guess I have the rhythmic equivalent of tone deafness. I don't even like to see other people dance. Maybe it just conjures up all that shyness I felt when I was thirteen. Joanne makes me dance one dance a year—threatens to get drunk and make a scene if I don't."

If dancing was never a part of the courtship, I'm not sure that a woman has the right to expect it later. The most unlucky women are those who thought they had married dancers. "They called him Jivin' Joe in college," said one woman about her husband. "He was the guy who'd get up on the stage with the band and dance the wildest dances. I loved it. I guess I didn't realize how much liquor it took for him to lose his inhibitions. We're grown-ups now. He can't drink that much anymore. And we hardly ever dance." Other men don't dance, I think, because dancing to music less earsplitting than that of our college days necessitates a little conversation. A lot of men are uncomfortable talking to women—even their own wives.

Perhaps the rising divorce rate has also taken its toll on dancing. I can't help believing that adult dances were more fun when marriages were less precarious. I can attest to the fact that there is great pleasure in dancing with the same man for sixteen years. Not only have we perfected our steps but dancing together also allows us to give each other our undivided attention, a luxury in a household with three children. It also reminds us of qualities in each other that we forget to admire in our daily lives. As one woman put it, "Last New Year's Eve we must have danced for a full three hours together, and after all these years and two babies, I came home in love all over again." I am perfectly content to dance the entire evening with my husband, but I also enjoy seeing him dance with other women, especially those who say to him, "Where have you been all my life? I haven't danced in twenty years." Nor does he have qualms about my other dancing partners. When marriages have some lasting quality, everybody can relax and enjoy the innocent flirtation that is inherent in dancing.

At recent social functions I have noted that only about a tenth of the men can be counted on to dance at all. It's hard to categorize them. My mother-in-law, who married a truly elegant dancer at a time when the big bands made dancing an essential ingredient in every courtship, says the best dancers she knew were tall, had excellent posture and were always gentlemanly. But I find few constant traits among the men I know who love to dance. One is shorter than I am, but women, including me, line up to dance with him. "I am the perfect height for any woman," he said. "I like to dance cheek to cheek or nose to bosom." He added, "I fell in love dancing—but then, I always fall in love dancing."

If these dancing men have any common trait, it is that they have learned that what women occasionally need, regardless of age or political philosophy, is not a pass but a little romance. And dancing is one way of fulfilling that need. They are the men at parties who light cigarettes, refill wineglasses and tell women they are beautiful. My father has been using the same corny line for fifty years— "Did anybody ever tell you you should have been in pictures?"—and I've never seen a woman who tired of hearing it.

I don't know what inspires men to become good danc-

ers these days. Almost all the men I talked with said that
their mothers had some hand in their learning to dance. I
hope it's not a genetic thing, something in the hippocam-
pus of the brain that determines whether one moves easily in space. I like to think that rhythm begins with singing
and rocking chairs in nurseries. As my father did with me,
I danced with my three sons long before their feet could
touch the floor. We have wild dance contests in the boys'
bedroom just before bedtime. And I enrolled the oldest
one in the slow-slow-quick-quick-slow dance classes at the
YMCA. I watched the little smart alecks arrive for the
class with their ties around their heads. "You just said we
had to wear a tie; you didn't say where." Later, on the way
home in the car, a mother heard them comparing notes:
"Janet's hand didn't sweat, but her other part sure did."
(Her other part, I think, is her waist.) It's hard to tell who's
going to take to it. I hope all three of mine do. So many
women are counting on it.

13 Some Day You'll Thank Me

"STRAIGHTEN UP or you'll find yourself attending the three-hour performance at SMU tonight!" I scribbled on a December church bulletin and dispatched it down the pew to my three sons. The tenor in the choir had just begun "Every valley shall be exalted," from Handel's *Messiah,* and my sons' suppressed giggling fit had built up to shoulder level, creating a seismic tremor in the pew. "The c-r-r-roo-ked straight, the c-r-r-roo-ked straight," enunciated the tenor, and one of my three made that snorting noise that inevitably erupts from attempts to cap the volcano of giggling that wells up when your wiseacre brother responds to his mother's reprimand with "Whose c-r-r-rew cut straight?"

I found that old church bulletin recently while putting away my winter purses, and I reluctantly confess that it's representative of the conversations I have had with my sons about music and the arts in general. Dorothy Parker once said, "You can lead a whore to culture but you can't make her think." I wish I could come up with an equally witty aphorism concerning my thwarted attempts to civilize my boys. You can take a child to a museum, concert or play, but you can't make him like it. You can't even make him look at it. I cannot erase the image of my oldest son sighing loudly as he stood in the middle of the room at the Dallas Museum of Fine Arts some years ago. His eyes were defiantly shut, and he asked every two minutes as I examined Renoir's *Luncheon of the Boating Party* from all angles, "Had enough yet, Mom?"

Equally vivid is my memory of the afternoon I took Drew to the Dallas Ballet's performance of *The Nutcracker*. Once we got past the opening Christmas party scene, Drew began asking, "When is somebody going to talk? This isn't going to be just dancing, is it?" I ignored him. All week I had conscientiously refrained from calling this *The Nutcracker* "ballet." When the snowflakes began their exquisite dance, he leaned over and asked in something more than a stage whisper, "What has happened to the plot of this story?" How could I tell him that all ballet plots are a little thin? Instead, I whispered angrily, "Would you rather go out and sit in the crime-ridden parking lot? I'm not leaving!" "No," he replied, "I'll stick around. There's one good part coming." With the penlight I had given him as a bribe for coming with me, he highlighted one word at the bottom of the program— "corps." "I hope it's Clara's," he said, grinning.

Under duress, all three boys accompanied me to the opening of the Dallas Museum of Art. Getting them into coats and ties midweek was asking too much, so I settled for school pants and shirts that buttoned. Even at that, one of them groused, "I can't believe it. The top of me looks like I'm going to Sunday school, and it's only Wednesday." The youngest asked if he could take his soccer ball.

John was out of town, so the boys were able to moan all the way downtown, "Daddy would never make us do this." They refuse to believe that their father ever initiates our visits to museums and galleries. "We can always turn Daddy to the 'dark side.' "

Then they begin a litany in praise of Daddy's dark side:

"If Daddy had a choice between King Tut and *Raiders of the Lost Ark,* which would he choose?"

"Raiders!!!!!"

"If Daddy had a choice between "Live from Lincoln Center" and the University of Houston versus Georgetown game, which would he choose?"

"Good-bye, Pavarotti, hello, Akeem Olajuwon."

Although I had visited the Dallas Museum of Art during its construction, I had failed to assess its design from a child's perspective. From the minute we entered, on the parking lot side, the race was on. The museum's broad limestone corridor, which sweeps the length of the building, makes running irresistible. "I knew I should have brought my soccer ball," William wailed as he escaped my grasp to catch up with his brothers, who were barreling at breakneck speed past *The Reveler* by Dubuffet.

I corralled them in the Gateway Gallery, the education wing. I knew something of the efforts that had gone into making this wing appealing and instructive to children. To ensure a participatory art experience, the area has a texture tunnel to crawl through, mirrored images to manipulate, a kaleidoscope to activate with sound, and "discovery boxes" to explore individually. Clowns and magicians on hand for the opening night, as well as the generally festive air, did not encourage the serious contemplation of art, but no one could say the kids weren't *participating.* Harry Parker, the museum director, had positioned himself there for the night, undoubtedly because he feared that the museum's insurance could not cover the loss of eyeballs as children careened around James Surls's spiky *Burning Dog.* The enormous soft

leather baseball glove envisioned as a cozy place for a
child to curl up and think about "line, mood, texture and
color" quickly became a landing pad for children who
shot out of the texture tunnel like projectiles. I lost my
three for a while, then caught up with them in the modern art gallery, where they were offering their scholarly
opinions on the collection.

"*Deep Forest Green Dispersion,* humph. Looks like a
worn-out pot scrubber."

"Stupid. I could do that. You call that art? Dumb."

I suddenly realized how sharply the battle lines are
drawn between us. I am definitely outmanned but not yet
outmaneuvered. At home the walls of their rooms are
clearly their own. The Barnum and Bailey posters and the
panda from the National Zoo have all been replaced by
posters of athletes: Bubba Smith ("Kill, Bubba, kill"), the
Globetrotters, Moses Malone shown parting a basketball
court, Dr. Dunkenstein, the Dallas Cowboys and an auto-
graphed picture of five wrestlers called the Von Erichs.
Jack's room is plastered with posters of motorcycles doing
absurdly dangerous stunts, a Texas Longhorn poster auto-
graphed by Fred Akers, and a map of the Big Bend.

But their bookshelves, with few exceptions, are full of
my aspirations. Besides the read-aloud books, they have
books on drawing and design and architecture, books with
color plates that trace the history of painting from
cavemen to the present, and small British Ladybird books
on Tudor kings and queens, Chinese civilization, and
Egyptian tombs. These books don't collect dust on the
shelf. My sons use twenty or thirty of them at a time to
create racetracks for small battery-powered Stomper 4x4
cars. I have watched forlornly as a Stomper with flashing
headlights clambered up *Favorite Tales from Shakespeare,* crossed *Doing Art Together,* slipped a bit on the

shiny cover of *Drawing from Nature,* and fell off the track
entirely at *What to Look for Inside a Church.* The encyclopedias, being uniform in size, are often employed as
walls for a gerbil maze.

For such ingrates, why do I frequently ruin my own
museum visits, pack my purse with candy bribes and even
then leave concerts during intermission? Perhaps because
I am at heart a nineteenth-century romantic who believes, as music educator Lowell Mason did, that through
"music you set in motion a mighty power which silently,
but surely, in the end, will humanize, refine and elevate a
whole community." I want them to learn to look, really
look, not just at art in museums but at trees on our block,
birds at the feeder, and the rainbow on the porch when
the sun hits the reflector on William's bicycle. I want them
to develop an active sense of their own aesthetic taste and
not be forever dependent on a polo pony logo to distin-
guish the "real" from the phony.

I want them to have in adult life something, in addition
to jogging, that allows them to escape the treadmill their
jobs may become. In accepting a National Book Critics
Circle Award, novelist John Updike said, "Whatever art
offered the men and women of previous eras, what it
offers our own, it seems to me, is space." He went on to
suggest that bookstores and museums should feel like the
vacant lots of childhood—places "where the spirit can
find exercise in unsupervised play." He reminded us that
encounters with art should leave us "astonished and star-
tled and at some deep level refreshed."

My family wakes up daily to the roar of Dallas' Central
Expressway, and I know my children will need those vacant lots. Their generation may know even more than
mine about creating life and destroying it, but I worry
that they won't know how to enhance it.

Our highly regarded public school in Highland Park has no compulsory arts education and very few field trips to operas, symphony performances or museums beyond the fifth grade. Education in music and art, subjects that are hard to measure on standardized tests, is still regarded as a frill that is necessarily ignored by many of the best high school students trying to cram in more courses that will count toward advanced placement in college. Has everybody forgotten that Einstein and Schweitzer were also musicians? Though my sons may have no artistic gifts to offer the world, they are growing up in a Texas city that has thriving museums, theaters, dance companies and music groups that deserve discriminating audiences. Mine should be the last generation of Texans who, out of ignorance, feel obliged to give standing ovations to every performer who condescends to grace our stages.

So much for my soapbox. I love my boys desperately, and I selfishly want them to be my companions and to share some of my interests in the brief years we have together. It is also the nature of middle-class parents to want for our children what we didn't have in our own childhoods.

No matter where a person grew up in Texas in the fifties, his exposure to the arts—especially the visual arts— is likely to have been severely limited. Of my elementary school art class, I remember only making a spool tray with a decal of a Mexican in serape and sombrero stuck in the corner. At the junior high level we lettered posters for the football team. The Baptist church I attended had a lovely stained-glass rose window at the back of the sanctuary, but when I was seated in a pew I could see only the glassed-in tank for total-immersion baptism. Sometimes we had a big cardboard thermometer indicating how much of the budget the tithing faithful had raised. At church camp one summer, I carved a rabbit out of Ivory soap, and to attain the rank of queen in the Baptist Girls' Auxiliary pageant, I cross-stitched a map of the world, using green thread for the "saved" portions and yellow for the heathen ones.

In music education I fared much better. My sons are being reared as Episcopalians, and I can't imagine how they'll employ a Sarum plainsong to rock their babies to sleep. I personally never met a cranky baby who wouldn't eventually succumb to the rhythm of "Bring them in, bring them in,/Bring them in from the fields of sin." In addition to the useful gospel fare, however, the classically trained choir director and organist gave me a fair dose of the great Christian oratorios—Haydn's *Creation*, Handel's *Messiah*, and Mendelssohn's *Elijah*—along with Mozart's *Requiem*. My sixth-grade teacher, Mrs. Holtzclaw, somehow found time to lead us through the stories and major themes and arias of three operas. I read the rest of the best-known opera plots while waiting for my piano lessons at Mr. Walters'. I was sixteen before I heard a live symphony performance. I was a sophomore in college before Donald Weismann's art history survey course at UT allowed me to see the relationships between art, music, history and philosophy.

I am undoubtedly misguided in my determination to make the things it's taken me forty years to learn so easily accessible all at once to my children. I've always loved the story of the small black boy in Philip Roth's *Goodbye, Columbus* who sneaks past the stone lions and the stuffy librarian to look at the "heart" section: "*Heart.* Man, pictures. Drawing books." On viewing a color print of a Gauguin—the one with three native women standing knee-deep in a rose-colored stream—he exclaims, "These people, man, they sure does look cool. They ain't no yelling or

shouting here, you could just see it. . . . *Look, look,* look
here at this one. Ain't this the f———ing *life?*" Such eu-
phoria of discovery is perhaps impossible for children who
are car-pooled from ballet class to art lessons, prodded
through museum texture tunnels and exhorted to notice
line, mood, color and period before moving briskly to the
next painting.

We're such amateurs at raising urban children. When I
related the art museum debacle to my husband, he was
properly sympathetic, but he also said, "You know I like to
go to museums from time to time, but it's not high on my
list of recreational activities."

"As a matter of fact," I said, "I've never quite forgiven
you for holing up in the *pensione* in Florence on our
honeymoon eighteen years ago with a James Bond thriller
while I trooped through the treasures of the early Italian
Renaissance wondering if I could stay married to a man
who would miss the Ghiberti doors."

"Now wait a minute," he protested. "I went with you
through so many cathedrals in Rome that I was beginning
to feel like St. Sebastian. I know how those boys feel. They
don't want to look at things. They want to do something."

"Yeah, they want to look at wrestling on TV and then
see if they can bang their own heads together," I countered.

Well, that isn't quite true. I've had some minor triumphs. Jack took a trip with me to Philadelphia and Washington a couple of years ago. I think the trip was remarkably successful because I made him the official
photographer. There was great status in adjusting the
shutter speed on his dad's 35mm camera in a crowd of
peers with Instamatics. Although he didn't give me much
favorable feedback at the Smithsonian or in the National

Gallery, his conversation reveals that he'll never forget the things he viewed so carefully through that lens.

I got my licks in on the second son early. While Drew was still a preschooler, a classmate's father visited the school and played the piano. He must have talked about the pleasure that playing gave him, even though he was not a professional musician. Drew came home announcing that he needed music lessons. I bet I found a teacher within the hour. When his initial interest waned, I bribed him with Slurpees from the 7-Eleven. Now, nearly six years later, as he rips through his scales and explains complicated rhythms to his mother, he will acknowledge only that the piano lessons have given him an edge in video games and basketball. ("I know how to use both hands independently," he brags.) He is also the most sensitive to my feelings and understands, though perhaps can't express it, why the Grieg Nocturne makes me cry.

My best hope, however, may be William, who will be alone with us for four years after the other two fly the coop. His drawings give him great pleasure, and if I can just keep his philistine older brothers off his back he may illustrate my first children's book. He and I have been to the new art museum four times now. These are secret, conspiratorial outings. We go as soon as he gets home from school, and we never tell his brothers where we've been. He took a school friend to the Shogun exhibit this spring. The little boys spent most of their time frightening museum guards with their quicksilver darting from display to display and talked of nothing but samurai swords that could stab your guts even in Shogun armor, but that night William kept the catalog in his room and drew tiny slant-eyed figures carrying palanquins and shiny lacquered boxes.

Until John's remark about preferring "to do something," it had never occurred to me to think of museums and concerts as passive experiences. Football games are passive experiences for me. I never played the game. I have no personal experience by which to measure what I'm seeing. My sons connect so easily with the visual poetry of a Laker-76er basketball game because they dribble and shoot basketballs for hours on the driveway. It has a lot to do with what you played or wanted to play as a child. I played the piano. And I wanted to draw. A kid who has had hands-on experience with a keyboard or a paintbrush doesn't emerge from a concert or a museum saying, "Dumb. I could do that."

"Exposure is the important thing at their age," my sage husband always counsels. "You can't expect them to like it. We just have to hang in there. Something is bound to stick."

Well, some of it has stuck, I suppose. Jack took art classes at the museum when he was eight. He never admitted that he enjoyed a minute of it, but years later, in an argument about my taste versus his, he screamed, "And I hate that art stuff—that Jackson Pollock with his splatter, splatter, splatter, that Picasso with his blue and red period, that Miró with those scribbles and kindergarten drawings, and that crazy one-eared van Gogh with all those wavy lines."

I could hardly suppress a smile. It was such a comforting inversion of the old saw, "I may not know much about art, but I know what I like." Jack may not know what he likes, but he knows a lot about art.

14 Kyrie Eleison

"Alleluia, joyful mother,
All thy children sing with thee."
—*Hymn 54, Hymnal of the
Protestant Episcopal Church,
1940*

SURELY IN the sweet by-and-by some special rewards will be handed out to parents who regularly took their recalcitrant children to church. I am banking on a few leisurely aeons of breakfasts in bed with the Sunday *Times* at least.

The last time my sons evidenced a glimmer of interest in things liturgical was at an Easter service several years ago. Just after a particularly triumphant trumpet fanfare, one turned, his eyes fairly dancing with anticipation, and whispered, "Is it going to be 'Star Wars'?"

My mind raced through the possibilities of theological parallels: "The prince of darkness grim . . . (Darth Vader) We tremble not for him." "Therefore with angels and archangels . . ." (Rebel forces?) Luke . . . yes, there's a Luke in this too. And a monster that swallows a man. No robots, but Moses knew something about special effects.

The exercise was futile. I spent the remainder of the

service seeing that starships made from the church bulletin were not launched over the edge of the balcony.

The boys never rise willingly on a Sunday morning, and we never pull out of the driveway to head for the church that one doesn't gaze forlornly at Rosie with her nose pressed at the front door pane and sigh, "If only I'd been born a dog."

We usually leave the house about 9:05, bound for the nine o'clock service. John and I are grinding our teeth from the ordeal of getting everyone dressed. A fight begun in the house resumes in the back seat: "Hit me, hit me . . . didn't hurt."

"Shut up, your breath is so bad, you'll cloud the communion wine."

"What about you, fang-gap tooth?"

"Look who's talking, wax ears."

Penitently John and I clamber with our brood into the latecomers' balcony. We lower the kneeler on Drew's foot and fall to our knees with the rest of the similarly encumbered late families whom we call "the last who shall someday be first." Oblivious to the new prayer book, I mumble the familiar words of the old General Confession: "We have left undone those things which we ought to have done." I think first of the unmade beds and dishes, then cock one eye open and wince at the left ear of the child dubbed "wax ears" in the car. Surveying the fingernails of the other two, I wonder if absolution can really be granted.

Back in our seats, John and I arrange ourselves so that all three boys are separated. Our church really is beautiful, and if I look neither to the left or right, the tranquillity is somewhat restorative. Some Sundays we share this pew with the director of the Dallas Art Museum and his family. Sitting beside them reassures me that, at the very least, my boys are probably absorbing a little architectural sense about Gothic arches, naves and transepts. Sitting beside the Parker family this particular Sunday is also comforting because the youngest of their four children, Katherine, has one foot squinched into a size 6 Mary Jane shoe while the other foot dangles a size 9. She will go sock-footed to the communion rail right behind my William, who has now attached his clip-on tie to his shirt pocket.

When we get to the Prayer of Humble Access: "Grant us therefore, gracious Lord, so to eat the flesh of thy dear Son Jesus Christ, and to drink his blood . . . ," also known to my sons as the cannibal prayer, the boys begin tugging at me and pointing with great embarrassment at their father. John, as usual, is reading this prayer about four words ahead of the rest of the congregation. I've tried to explain to them that Daddy reads at a fast clip because he grew up embarrassed by his Scottish grandfather who, as a retired Episcopal priest, always read with full brogue in stentorian tones about a paragraph behind the congregation.

Once we get to the longer eucharistic prayers, my three make no pretense of participating. They reach for the self-adhesive visitors' cards in the back of the pew. The Parker children make interesting cubist constructions out of theirs. My boys once made shepherds' beards by sticking the narrow cards on their chins, but ordinarily they just write "Kick me" or "Dumby" and surreptitiously stick them on one another's backs as we file down the aisle for communion. I mutter some threats about decorum as they proceed, but once out of my reach, Drew stuffs his hands in his pockets and saunters, while Jack walks close behind him, treading deliberately on Drew's heels and causing him to trip out of his shoes in full view of the congregation.

The communion rail itself has more potential for disaster. I have seen wafers chewed, then spit back in hands for closer examination. Sometimes, despite my lectures, they walk back down the aisle with index fingers raking the wafer out of the roofs of their mouths. For years one did a gagging routine after receiving the wine. Now he just staggers, insisting the sip has made him tipsy. Most original performance, however, goes to the child, not mine, who smuggled a musical key ring to the altar, so that interspersed with the plainsong "Humbly, I adore thee, verity unseen . . ." we also got a tinkly rendition of "Lara's Theme" (Somewhere my love . . .") from *Dr. Zhivago.*

Nevertheless, we return from communion filled and, despite the fact that William trampled the calves of the man kneeling beside us as we made our getaway, we feel forgiven. After all, didn't Jesus say something about "Except ye be a child . . ."?

We are not yet well suited for solemn occasions. Our family's chronic sinusitis defiles our pew with tissue snowfall, and on one occasion I lost a half slip with exhausted elastic as we dashed in the church door. I have knelt more than once, heard a giggle and felt my unzipped skirt gape.

"We are not getting anything out of this, Mother," Jack usually pleads midway through the service. I take solace in the fact that William has momentarily stopped drawing swastikas and bombers on the bulletin. He is clearly drawing a chalice which, in case I don't recognize it, he labels "Whine Cup." Drew recently conceded that Sunday school had helped him a lot in Trivial Pursuit.

But sometimes it *is* hard to see what they're getting out of this weekly experience. My boys do not long for "newness of life." They are seldom penitent or even aware of their transgressions. At an Easter service they squirm and jerk at their tight collars. "It's too hot in here." "It's too boring," they sigh. I look at the lilies on the altar and the trumpets and wonder how the promise of hope and the banishment of despair become pertinent to a male child.

A young priest at the church confessed that not one of the youth group at a recent football game could identify the biblical reference on that ubiquitous banner displayed at games that says simply John 3:16. ("For God so loved the world, that he gave his only begotten Son, that whosoever believeth in him should not perish, but have everlasting life.") I quizzed my boys after I heard that to see if they knew the scripture. Drew's eyes lit up. "Oh, I know, I know . . ." he said. "It has something to do with football." With such Talmudic scholars as these older brothers, small wonder that William believes Moses' last name was Malone and Abraham's Lincoln. In one of our cosmic discussions of "When did it all begin?" I reminded William of the Bible story "In the beginning . . ." "Oh, I know that one," he reassured me. I was momentarily relieved until he proceeded to relate a tale of a guy stealing fire and getting chained to a mountain where eagles ate his liver. Drew, particularly restless during a long baptismal service, once passed me a note that said, "Can't we find a church that worships Zeus? He's much more interesting." Beware of proselytizing ancient Greeks.

Obviously I am not Susannah Wesley. We have indeed left undone several things which we ought to have done. That's one reason we persevere in the church attendance. It is a discipline, and we have so little of that in our lives. The same young priest who accompanied the kids to the football game says that each Sunday he tries very hard to read the liturgy perfectly. I appreciate his effort. I like to think that on a Sunday the whole catholic and apostolic Church offering in global display this Great Thanksgiving in perfect unison must give God some pleasure. "On the other hand," I assured the priest, "don't worry if you miss a word or two. We sinners take a lot of comfort in a slightly flubbed eucharist." A little wine spilled on a chasuble may be what connects the Lord's Table to my own. I once saw a priest accidentally tilt the tray, spilling all of the hosts on the carpet. He knelt for the next prayer, surreptitiously scooted them all back on the tray and fed them to us. When guests weren't looking, I've done the same thing with the dinner rolls at my house.

We can't even get grace before meals right. For all of the "beams" in our own eyes, children are bent on perfection, especially in the behavior of their siblings. If it is William's turn to say grace, he inevitably begins, "God is good. . . ."

"Ernk!" chorus the barracuda brothers.

"Hush," I say. "Maybe he's saying one you haven't heard."

"God is good . . . uh . . . uh," he continues.

("Okay, William," I silently cheer, "go on. 'God is great . . .' You can finish in style if you add, 'Let us thank you for this plate.' ")

He can't go on. His brothers are giggling. He is crying.

"Quiet!" John roars.

We roust them out of bed on Sunday mornings for other reasons too. John and I both have religious resonances from our own childhoods that we cannot escape. His stem from being the grandson of a priest and from four years in an Episcopal boarding school with the motto *Nisi Dominus Frustra* (Except the Lord build the house, they labor in vain that build it. Psalms 127). Mine, on the other hand, are distinctly East Texas Southern Baptist. Few churches have ever absorbed more of the time and energy of its members than the First Baptist on Pine Street in Texarkana did in the fifties. I regularly logged about six or seven hours on Sunday and at least three on Wednesday. I was a little achiever who loved getting gold stars on memory verse charts. I knew exactly what my geometry teacher meant when, in exasperation at our inability to recall yesterday's theorem, he threw the chalk and yelled, "It's just Hebrews 13 and 8 . . . Hebrews 13 and 8." ("Jesus Christ, the same yesterday, today and forever.") My father, who occasionally mentioned his family in his Sunday newspaper column, dubbed me The Little Missionary and my brother The Prodigal Son. The Prodigal was among the first to discover that one could drink Cokes at the Grim Hotel pharmacy a block from the church instead of going to Sunday school. The Little Missionary once poured a Christmas fifth of Johnny Walker Red Label down the kitchen sink. Hating to see the preacher lose out in the weekly soul-winning count, some of us felt compelled to volunteer for the mission field. I think I was eleven when I decided during altar call to surrender all my talents for use in darkest Africa or India, snatching the heathen from the pits of hell. The Prodigal, sitting with my parents in the pew near the front of the church, immediately put his hands to either side of his head and with rapid tongue movements made a face like a hooded cobra. He said later that he wanted to be sure that I knew the perils of the territory I was volunteering for. When I reneged on the promise to go to India, I suppose I took refuge in the Episcopal Church. In college, I was converted as much by Thomas Cranmer's prayer book as by the priest who quoted G. K. Chesterton as frequently as St. Paul.

However, my Episcopal-reared children know that I still view their paltry biblical knowledge with Baptist alarm. I can't fathom their making it through the perils of childhood without some talismans. If they have nightmares after seeing *Indiana Jones and the Temple of Doom,* they know that I will prescribe the Twenty-third Psalm. Summer skies in the Texas hill country are grander if somewhere in your head rings "The heavens declare the glory of God; and the firmament showeth his handiwork." And death, especially the death of their great-grandfather, requires "Let not your heart be troubled: ye believe in God, believe also in me. In my Father's house are many mansions: if it were not so, I would have told you." Beneath any pseudosophistication, anxiety, layers of doubt and rationalizations, we are believers.

Finally, we go to church Sunday after Sunday out of a need to say "thank you" for inordinate and inexplicable blessings—healthy children and a good marriage. Judith Martin (Miss Manners) has written that "getting children to say thank you directly and in writing is one of the chief tasks of child rearing. It is a simple matter requiring about ten years of constant vigilance, but those who give up on it might as well concede failure on the entire enterprise of civilizing their young." Prayer seems to contain levels of gratitude that we can't express any other way.

We tie their neckties in the car, and they protest all the way down Cole Avenue that their friends are at home watching wrestling on TV. I see enough of that at church.

15   *Brotherhood*

WHEN MY friend Sarah gave birth to her second son I wrote to her, "I know you wanted a girl, but after observing my three sons, it's hard for me to imagine how your Jacob would grow up without at least one brother. Boys seem to thrive on a sort of rivalry that most females would find ridiculous or just counterproductive. It's sometimes helpful to regard them as less highly developed creatures —trilobites or nematodes. John says that's too harsh. He prefers to think of them as wolf cubs who express affection by chewing each other's ears off. However, the blank, uncomprehending, disinterested stares they give in response to my lectures on the need for tolerance are clearly pre-mammal. Don't expect instant male bonding. Mine are Three Musketeers only if the motto reads: 'Free-for-all, and Two Against One.' Gird your loins."

I hope I didn't frighten her. As my boys have grown older, the rivalry *has* become more subtle. It's been two years since we returned from an evening out and found the door to Drew's bedroom propped against his wall. Uncharacteristically, every boy was in his bed with lights out. On closer examination, the center panel of the door was splintered and the hole was a brother-shaped silhou-

ette. I guessed the familiar scenario immediately. Taunt
and run, taunt and run, slam door to bedroom just as big
brother careens around the corner—BLAM! At least it
scared them into their beds. Contrition is quite another
matter. When I meted out the punishment and assessed
them for the damages, I heard somebody mutter, "That
door never did that before. How were we to know?"

Nevertheless, the repaired door and all of our doors are
reasonably secure on their hinges. These days the attack is
more verbal and psychological. It is a one-upmanship vali-
dated by some infuriating slang like "Burned you . . .
ooooh, smoked him" or "Snag . . ." For months the put-
downs were accompanied by a hand not quite slapping
the face of the humiliated and an accompanying mouth
sound like the surf roaring, which I suppose indicated that
a wave had just wiped him off the face of the earth.

The intense rivalry is undoubtedly fueled by the diver-
sity of personalities in this house. I've had some hand in
that. A television talk show host once asked me how I
handled the scene in the grocery store when my child
threw a tantrum in front of the gum counter. "Which
child?" I asked. With Jack, I think we left the store and sat
in the car where I "mirrored" his feelings. ("I know you
want the gum. Gum is fun to chew, but it's not good for
your teeth," etc.) With Drew in tow, I whacked him publicly and yelled angrily, "No gum." With William, the
baby, I bought the gum. They are still working out these
inequities in their upbringing.

Jack is fastidious and well organized. His hair is always
combed and parted. His bed is made, his schoolbooks perfectly covered, and his desk is cleared daily. His hamster's
cage is cleaned once a week without my asking. He's been
this way since birth. In a household so rarely ordered, his
room is an island of tranquillity. When he was just old

enough to dress himself, he began laying out his clothes in a pattern we dubbed "The Little Man": shirt with arms extended, jeans with belt already in the loops, and shoes and socks extending from each pant leg. He is the only contact lens wearer I know who has never, ever skipped one step of the ritual cleansing recommended by the optician.

Drew, on the other hand, once surveyed the chaos of his room and said, "I just love it this way. It's full of surprises. See that pile of pajamas? Last night a cat's paw reached out of that and snagged me on the ankle just like in the jungle." Birds and squirrels he knows by name come to his window and the dog and her fleas sleep on his seldom-made bed. His allowance is always docked, but his wants are few. For pocket change, he walks Osso, a huge black dog on our block that most children are scared of. His homework seems to get done at the breakfast table, which explains the syrup stains. His shoes are untied and his hair seldom combed. His nails would grow like a Chinese mandarin's if his music teacher and I didn't intervene. He is a left-handed basketball player and sports-statistic nut. Old sports pages collect beside his bed and gum wrappers litter his nightstand drawer. In a Chinese restaurant, his fortune cookie more than once has read, "Family harmony depends on you." And it does. Despite the clutter of his life, he rarely seems depressed and has never sustained a pout or held a grudge. He is spontaneously affectionate and still kisses his mother in public. He once wrote a letter to "Dr. J" (Julius Erving) and after mailing it, remarked, "It just feels so good to know that somebody so important is going to read my letter and think about me." If I yell at him to get his schoolbooks and coat off the kitchen floor, he sings out, "You and Betty Crocker can BAKE SOMEONE HAPPY. . . ."

However, like his siblings, he does love a good tag team match, and he is often the catalyst for major imbroglios. When life is too tranquil, Drew knows he can always incite a riot by casually tweaking William on the nose. This is known as a nose honk and is considered a particularly good "smoke" on William since his nose is growing faster than the rest of him and threatens to become a replica of his father's flaring Super Chief.

William is the easiest pickings in the pecking order. He relishes his position as the blue-eyed baby of the family. "Jack and Drew grabbed any old brown eyes up in heaven just to get here first. I hung around for the beautiful ones and got all of the angel kisses [freckles] too," he confides dreamily before he drifts off to sleep. The independence his older siblings sought so young is not so appealing to this last child of mine. Shoe tying and eventually reading in the first grade seemed like unnecessary hurdles for William. As he knowingly pointed out, "I like the books you read to me, Mom. The ones I can read are so dumb." With some dismay, I discovered that he had settled happily at school into the reading group with the non-English-speaking children.

His brothers, like a pair of interfering childless aunts, incessantly kibitz. "You baby him, Mom. At his age, we were franchising lemonade stands. He can't even cross Hillcrest Ave.," one says. "He's just like the cat," says the other. "You have to knock him off the table or he'll never learn." "He backwashes when he drinks his milk, Mother, it's disgusting," Jack informs me. "William," they taunt, "don't talk with your mouth open."

Maybe I have babied him. I thought I was just salvaging a bit of childhood for a little boy whose fantasies are always being preempted or held up to ridicule. At three years, William went to the theater with his brothers to see his first movie, *The Empire Strikes Back,* probably the most violent of George Lucas' trilogy. I remember gripping his tiny hand in the dark and thinking, "This child hasn't even seen *Bambi.*" To assuage my guilt, he and I went to see *Bambi* by ourselves weeks later. When we returned, his brothers pounced unmercifully. "Did he cry? Did he cry? A little sweaty around the eyes, Willie?"

"No, he didn't cry," I told them. "What did you expect from a child who witnessed a creature being eviscerated and a man being frozen to death two weeks ago?"

"Aw, Mom, he just didn't understand *Bambi,*" they groaned. "William," Drew said, overenunciating, "the mother died. Bambi's mother got killed. Didn't you get it? No more Mommy for Bambi."

"So?" shrugged the jaded three-year-old.

On the kindergarten achievement test, when William rhymed the words "meat" and "leaf," I tried to explain to the teacher that his brothers never allowed him to watch "Sesame Street" because it conflicted with "Batman." They made fun of him when he curled up in my lap to read "Hickety, pickety, my black hen." He delighted more in their parodies of Mister Rogers than the real thing, and consequently he went off to school armed with words like "faggot" and "farthead," but a little fuzzy on the days of the week.

To make matters worse, Jack and Drew regularly feed him absurd misinformation. "Broccoli grows in the armpits of owls," they advise him at the dinner table. They went to great pains to teach him that he would always know his age by counting the fingers on his hand. "Count 'em, Willie. One, two, three, four, five. See, you're five years old. Next year you'll grow another one." I don't know how far into his sixth year he watched for the new finger. For several summers they set him up in a lemonade stand on our very lucrative corner. With his baseball cap turned backward, his freckles and the dog, Willie was terrific bait. The brothers, of course, confiscated most of his profits by teaching him that shiny round coins were more valuable than green paper bills.

Our attempts to come to his aid have invariably backfired. One Christmas John bought William a Texas Instruments Speak 'N Read, with hopes that it might interest him in learning to read independently. When a correct answer was recorded, the small toy computer responded in mechanized nasal tones, "You remembered one." William understood the voice to say, "You remembered Len." His brothers have never forgiven that ERROR, and when other taunts fail, they can usually reduce him to tears with "Hey, Willie, remembered Len lately? How's he doin'?"

Similarly, when he was five, he emerged from Sunday school class with a red doilied heart on which he had laboriously printed, "I Love Bems." I was puzzled, but admired it and tried to stuff it in my coat before his brothers joined us. Poor William retrieved the artwork and displayed it proudly to his brothers. "William-loves-bems, William-loves-bems," they singsonged all the way to the church parking lot. Tears streaming down his cheeks when we got in the car, he took a pen from my purse and carefully changed the Valentine to read, "I Hat Bems." He will never live that one down.

Clearly, William gets the worst of it. Even Drew the tormentor regularly reminds us, "Childhood isn't what it used to be in this family." But the competition between Jack and Drew is inherently more intense. Innocent nose honks can quickly escalate into brutal punches when those two are involved. Two years apart in age, they are at twelve and fourteen almost equals in size and verbal acu-

ity. Jack seizes gleefully on every evidence of Drew's
slothfulness. He treasures a snapshot he took of Drew
from the upstairs window. In the picture, Drew is sitting
contentedly in a garbage can amid the piles of leaves he is
supposed to be raking. Jack's favorite fantasy is of Drew
being sent off to military school. He charges Drew rent on
shirts they share and regularly flings Drew's possessions
left on the third floor down the stairwell. It confounds
Jack that there is almost no way to make Drew miserable.

Drew even takes Jack's teasing about his music lessons
in stride. He responds with infuriating imitations of Jack
talking to adults on the telephone in what Drew calls his
phony "Mr. Nice Guy" voice. For all of his hammy retorts,
Drew covets Jack's approval and friendship more than
either knows. Those years of trailing worshipfully as a
toddler behind his invincible big brother who made him
grow up too fast have not dimmed even as the gap between them has narrowed. "Did you hear Jack cheering
for me at my basketball game?" Drew asks, more excited
about his brother's encouragement than the final score.

The three of them seldom—no, never—acknowledge
the advantages they offer one another. The younger two,
of course, have benefited immeasurably from having Jack,
the "experimental" firstborn, go first. He scrutinizes their
wardrobes, their haircuts, and keeps them abreast of the
latest fads. Over my strong objection, Jack talked his father into including Drew in a rock concert outing. Without Jack's persistence, Drew would never have ridden a
moped in Mexico. William's and Drew's dueling with this
perfectionist has toughened their hides. Tell Jack the biggest event of your day, and he may say, "Got a quarter?
Go call someone who cares." Surely the world cannot be
any harsher than this big brother.

Jack and Drew also provide each other constant com-

panionship. Someone is always available for throwing
footballs, Frisbees or for shooting baskets. Three boys in
one household not only constitute a crowd, they usually
attract one. Count the bicycles in front of our house on
any weekend. It's hardly ever necessary to formally
orchestrate activity around here.

Without my asking and without my permission, Jack
and Drew have allowed William to tag along to their
friends' houses. As soon as he mastered his tiny two-
wheeler, he frequently accompanied them through terrible traffic to off-limits convenience stores or sandwich
shops. Perhaps they thought he'd "squeal" if they left him
behind. Once when Grandmother was baby-sitting, they
gave her the afternoon off while they took William to a
PG-13 movie at the neighborhood theater. While I offi-
cially disapprove of most of these outings, I have not forgotten the elation I felt at being included in my big brother's teenage crowd when I was only seven. Perhaps it's
only in conspiracy against the common enemy (me) that
they will learn to love and help each other.

"I'll bet you wish you had different children," Jack says
uneasily after a particularly contentious dinner which
seems to disturb no one's digestion except mine.

"Oh, I sometimes wish for a daughter, but just think
what I would have missed if I didn't have you." Daughters
would probably never give me a Mother's Day card
signed with first and last names. A girl might not think to
make a science project out of old sandwiches left in her
locker. (Peanut butter on white bread is eternal. Tuna on
whole wheat is transient.) If I had daughters, I would
never have known what happens in boys' gym classes. I
will never reveal it to his mother, but I know the name of
the child who has distinguished himself by hitting the
urinal from the farthest point. "You wouldn't know about

this, Mom, but people in gym class really have no decency at all," one tells me. I am so immersed now in their male perspective that I catch myself from time to time regarding my own sex with disloyal objectivity. I shrink from the shrillness in women's voices and feel the panic in a small boy's heart when a particularly garrulous mother approaches our car in the car-pool line. I told a group of women friends that I thought we should probably curtail the amount we talk by about one third during each remaining decade.

Without sons, I would never have feared war in such a personal way. All three after nightmares have asked, "Would you let them make me go fight and kill somebody?" Small wonder that boys cling so tenaciously to their childhoods.

Nor would I have observed the peculiar nature of male friendship. Two of my boys spent their elementary school years with no real best friend at all. And even now that they all seem to have friends, they know so little about each other. The whole point of male friendship seems to be "doing," not talking about who or what you like, not talking at all, just action. By contrast, at their ages, I could have told you my best friend's favorite color, favorite movie star, the best book she'd ever read, the kind of dress she'd buy if her mother would let her, the color of her room, her bedspread, the wish she'd wish if an eyelash fell on her cheek, what makes her cry, the two boys in our class she'd like to marry and what she intended to name her babies. The unrelenting competitiveness among boys, and perhaps men, precludes the consoling, vulnerable conversations that females have from an early age.

Boys only write to their brothers and friends at camp under duress. This single letter from Jack came home in the bottom of Drew's camp trunk:

Dear Drew,

Greg and I went up to University Cycle and got a catalog. It's got the new Predators. I found out Jim's bike
STINKS! His is called CroMo Free. (I'm not talking about
his racing bike.) His regular bike is a street bike. I've
picked out a bike for you. It's a Predator Team Alloy/Z
for $244.95. It's got everything. Double clamp, Sugino
GT three piece cranks, Sanshin alloy hubs, Dia-Comp
MX900 brakes, fluted alloy seat post.

                                                    Jack

This is all he had to say to a brother he hadn't seen for
three and a half weeks? It may be all his brother wanted to
hear.

I have to believe that they are communicating in ways I
don't understand. When we have dinner out together,
they frequently finish eating long before John and me.
Excused from the table, they race outside the restaurant.
There's something tender about the way Jack instinctively holds William's hand in unfamiliar territory. Sometimes I look up from my plate to see them at the large
restaurant window. They are holding hands and simulat-
ing a wave-breaking sequence with their arms or sometimes just striking their old standby "See No Evil, Hear No
Evil, Speak No Evil" monkey pose. While I feign embarrassment, I secretly applaud almost any activity that
seems to unite these disparate beings.

"One fall, winner take all," John yells as all three circle
him on his knees on our bedroom carpet at night. They
giggle nervously, waiting to pounce on him. The stated
object of this tag team match is to pin John's shoulders to
the floor by sitting on his chest for the count of three. It is
also a chance for some sort of primal physical contact that

I don't pretend to understand. There is some hugging, some gritting of teeth and surely some working out of pent-up hostilities. They become a mass of arms and legs. "Get him, Jack," Drew yells. "Hold him, Willie." Rosie is as confused as I am by the scene. She thinks her charges are in distress and nips at their flanks to try to extricate them. It is a quintessential male experience—noisy, physical, competitive, and by their account so much fun. They will remember it with far more fondness than my fireside chats.

Once, after viewing one of those sentimental "Reach out and touch someone" telephone commercials, I turned to Jack and said, "You know, someday when you're all grown up, your phone is going to ring and you'll be so glad to hear your brother's voice."

"Yeah, I probably will," he agreed, "especially if the operator says the call is from Australia."

16

Many Happy Reruns

I HAVEN'T given many spectacular birthday parties for my sons. It's just one more area where mothers of sons seldom excel. We scan the newspaper feverishly a week before the event in search of some Don Knotts retrospective film festival which will placate the boy who insists that anything tamer than the *Texas Chainsaw Massacre* will not keep his friends entertained. Mothers of sons were probably the primary investors in the pizza parlors and indoor amusement parks that offer full birthday party services on *their* premises.

Invitations to boys' parties may omit the address, but they always specify the time when the party is over. As a veteran of several at-home birthday parties, I encourage parents of guests to keep their car engines idling out front since boys seem to be able to tear open presents, play two dumb games, blow out candles on the cake, eat two bites of icing (I never served ice cream after the first party experience) and adjourn to break the honoree's new toys in less than half an hour.

Jack and Drew can't recall anything about the parties I gave them as preschoolers. Actually, Drew has never had a significant party, since his August birthday invariably falls during the week we spend at the beach on Padre

Island. One year I do remember buying a wonderful Batman piñata in a Mexican market and hanging it from the light fixture in our rented condominium. I was so fond of the piñata that I couldn't bear to see it banged to smithereens, so I attached a grocery bag full of candy to its foot. In the home movies, he is now dubbed Batman with catheter bag.

I also have movies of a magician sawing Jack's head off on his seventh birthday, but Jack has only a vague recollection of it. I remember that party, not because the magic tricks were so grand, but because Drew, probably disgruntled at the excessive attention lavished on Jack, hid so well in the thick hedge in our backyard that we reported him missing to the neighborhood police.

William's birthday might be forgotten entirely if it didn't fall so close to Thanksgiving. We made the Thanksgiving family feast his party for the first four years. At five, we hired Mr. Green, an ageless clown who is entertaining the children of children he delighted thirty years ago. His routine is guaranteed to give any adult present a headache, but children never seem to tire of his nonstop silliness. At William's party he stuck faucets on his bald head, took the honoree's picture with a squirt camera and said "poo-poo" a lot. When my older boys looked in on the scene he made them wear googly-eyed glasses and sing "Yankee Doodle." Except for two guests who fell off their chairs giggling, Mr. Green kept them all seated long enough for me to clear the gift debris and serve the cake. Since it was rainy and cold outside that day, I would not have balked had he doubled his fee.

However, with Jack and Drew old enough to be my assistants, I decided to give more thought to William's party last year. We'd have no more paid entertainers and no more homogenized parties in food franchise party rooms.

This third son has always been more receptive to fantasy than his older brothers ever were. First, I composed a letter to him from the ghost who inhabits our old house. Shortly after we moved in we named her Mrs. Murray in honor of our house's first owner. She is a pleasant ghost who does her entertaining downstairs while we're asleep. While she frequently appropriates our favorite pens, car keys, glasses and sock mates, she returns all except the socks within a day or two. We've talked about her so often that one morning when I rose at five to catch an early plane I honestly felt I was intruding in her kitchen. On another morning Drew unnerved us all by opening and shutting the downstairs powder-room door while exclaiming, "Oh, excuse me, Mrs. Murray."

For William's birthday letter, it seemed entirely plausible that Mrs. Murray should write in shaky scrawl about her pirate grandfather who had spent his last years puttering in her garden. She hinted strongly that a treasure map might be buried there. The game was afoot.

The older boys helped me devise rhyming clues that would take William and his cronies from digging holes in the backyard to seeking clues tucked in *Treasure Island* at the public library. Drew deposited other clues in cut tennis balls along a rocky ledge in the park near our house. Hot dogs appeared in a clearing and the ultimate treasure, heaps of foil-wrapped bubble gum money and hideous Mr. T jewelry, had to be unearthed near the creek. It was a hard act to follow.

This year I tried to interest William in taking his friends to a dramatic performance of *Tales from the Arabian Nights* being held at the museum auditorium in nearby Fort Worth. He had loved the stories and had drawn and painted magic carpets and Ali Baba's cave at his art class the month before. "I just couldn't, Mom," he wailed.

"They'd hate it. Let's just go to Chuck E. Cheese for pizza and video games."

His brothers greeted my *Arabian Nights* idea with similar enthusiasm. "Just give him what he wants, Mom: a G. I. Joe party."

A G. I. Joe party? I was once a pacifist mother who allowed no toy guns in her yard. By the time William was born I relented on water pistols. Somehow, in the past couple of years, all of William's hand-me-down Creative Playthings have been traded. In their stead is a toy box full of plastic Lugers, M-16s, bayonets, Uzis and a camouflage jump suit. From nowhere his small friends converge, all wearing OD green with camo helmets, laced-up boots and backpacks. They wage guerrilla warfare from my trees and hedges and retreat to a lean-to campsite they've built against a neighbor's fence.

Feeling thoroughly compromised, I headed to the Army-Navy surplus store in search of gifts and party favors. I found sergeants' stripes for thirty-five cents, a Marine T-shirt with a snarling bulldog on the front, a canteen and belt, a linty Army blanket and a Special Forces beret.

On the day of William's birthday he received a TOP SECRET message which I had composed with Drew's help:

TOP SECRET

TO: Special Forces headquartered on Beverly Drive

FROM: General Cragsnort, Dept. of the Army, Special Birthday Celebration Division

YOUR MISSION TODAY IS A DANGEROUS ONE. ITS PURPOSE IS TO SECURE THE AREA FOR PROPER BIRTHDAY

CELEBRATIONS. I HAVE SENT THIS TOP SECRET COMMU-
NIQUE BY A TRUSTED VILLAGER KNOWN TO YOU AS
DREW. HE KNOWS THE TERRAIN AND WILL ACT AS
YOUR GUIDE.

YOU ARE TO PROCEED TO ARMSTRONG BRIDGE [behind
the school], CHECK THE BRIDGE FOR EXPLOSIVES, THEN
SEARCH THE AREA TO INTERCEPT ENEMY TRANSMIS-
SIONS WHICH MAY BE HIDDEN IN A TENNIS BALL.

THE ENEMY MESSAGE WILL BE IN CODE. ATTACHED IS
OUR CODE DECIPHERING TEAM'S MOST RECENT CODE
BOOK.

GOOD LUCK,

Gen. Ozymandias P. Cragsnort

The deciphered codes directed William and his guests
to the park again, where Drew led them on maneuvers
across the creek, up a hill, and across the treacherous
ledge. At his command they made a shaky descent from
the ledge by shinnying down a small tree. More inter-
cepted messages led them to the abandoned enemy camp
where they feasted on the enemy's rations. Down the
trail, they took their first prisoner, our favorite teddy bear
dressed in Foreign Legion gear. They searched him for
maps, confiscated his candy cigarettes, had a "smoke" and
tied him to the cold drink cooler. The map ultimately led
them to a rusty ammo box jammed in the limestone wall
above the creek. When opened, the box revealed Special
Forces medals and foil-wrapped chocolate coins. We returned to the house for a birthday cake that only a boy
could love. A green plastic tank clambered over snowy
frosting past birthday-candle flares toward brown candy

rocks which hid plastic troops crawling on their bellies amid jelly-bean shrapnel.

That night as I tucked the birthday warrior in for the night I lingered a minute to ask, "Willie, what was the best surprise of the whole party?"

He didn't even hesitate. "The biggest surprise was when I opened that G. I. Joe Watchtower from Grant."

Too bad I didn't get this party on the home movies. Instant replay might make it memorable.

17

Crossing into Forty

THE HANDSOME man sitting across from me in the Dallas Love Field airport lounge looked vaguely familiar. English 301, "Beowulf to Burns"? No, maybe Professor Archie Lewis' Byzantine history? Blind date to SAE matched party? I hoped not.

Our flight to Houston was delayed, so I occupied myself as I often have at this airport by trying to identify former college classmates. There were at least five thousand students in my graduating class at the University of Texas. Of course I didn't know them all but, of those I did know, the majority seemed to have settled in Houston. The odds on seeing someone I'd known in the early sixties at this particular airline terminal, especially during the commuting hours, were always high.

The man looked up from his newspaper before I diverted my stare. He smiled as if he recognized me too, and before I could come up with his name he extended his hand and said, "Mrs. Mackintosh, I'll bet you don't remember me, I'm Jack Crump. You taught me when I was in the eighth grade."

Ooooh. Well, I *am* forty. My college classmates are flash frozen in my mind at twenty-one. I am shocked that we can all say, "Twenty years ago . . ." and be referring to our adult lives. At the airport now, I must remember that the men with gray or thinning hair, slightly paunchy waistlines and comfortable if not jowly faces are my contemporaries.

My women friends are another matter entirely. Arriving at a dance club party recently, my husband, who believes his contemporary, former Dallas Cowboy quarterback Roger Staubach, will soon tire of Rolaids and real estate and make a comeback, jokingly greeted three lovely women at the door with "You are all so well preserved. If I didn't know what natural beauties you are, I'd think you'd all had face lifts." To his chagrin, later in the evening he learned that two of the three *had*. Nevertheless, as I looked around the party, even by candlelight, we were all clearly somebody's parents. We have known cancer, divorce, errant children and middle-aged crazies. When we order a drink, the waiter isn't going to ask for an ID.

I don't mind being forty; I'm just not sure I'm qualified. Forty-year-old women, in my mind's eye, are the utterly sophisticated women Richard Avedon photographed in the forties and fifties. They are self-possessed and they know how to smoke seductively. How can I be forty when I still see suits and hats in better stores that are clearly too old for me?

Some of my adult accomplishments have recently become obsolete. I can make a roux. I can fry a chicken and make cream gravy as well as Lilla Gray, the black woman who cooked for my aunt twenty years ago. It took me years to master an "over easy" fried egg. My children, of course, prefer franchise fried food, and for the sake of our arteries, I must now learn to poach and steam.

However, if my capabilities and sophistication don't

seem quite ready for this crossing, clearly my face and attitudes must reflect the candles on the cake. I am steeled to the summer law clerk in my husband's office who said as a sincere compliment at dinner, "You know, you remind me so much of my mom." Later in the evening, when I decried the fact that my old college sorority had recently made an alumnae appeal for funds to enlarge the TV room, the young clerk's date silenced me with "Well, Mrs. Mackintosh, you know soap operas are far more important in people's lives than they were in *your* day."

My day? I stifled the impulse to tell her that, while I had never seen "General Hospital," I *had* danced with wild abandon to the Rolling Stones. Was that the only experience that she and I had in common? My unair-conditioned childhood without TV, even my college days with curfews and flickering black and white television for watching the Kennedy funeral, have become as quaint to those young adults as my father's reminiscences of Model Ts were to me.

And if young adults find me quaint, my own children must listen to their father's and my tales of yore with amused incredulity.

"Okay, Dad," they taunt, "tell us again about the time your mother forgot to pick you up at school for the Yankee exhibition game in Austin and it broke your heart." They are, from our small-town perspective, sated, urban children who take artichokes, live theater and major league baseball too much for granted. They think they've seen my childhood on TV sitcom reruns.

"Did I ever tell you about Oley the bus driver?" I ask.

"Gee, Wally, beats me." They shrug.

Some of my reminiscences must seem as remote to them as "Little House on the Prairie." "Well, Oley weighed about three hundred pounds and gave me free rides on his bus all over the neighborhood. He even parked the city bus at my corner to bring me a birthday present."

"Probably a child molester," my worldly-wise cynics chorus.

I persist and tell them about Halloween at Mrs. Mays's house where all of the treats were homemade—popcorn balls, brownies, caramel apples. "She made us print our names in her special book so we couldn't 'trick or treat' her house more than once during the evening." My sons have grown up believing that all homemade Halloween goodies contain razor blades or rat poison. How nice it was to grow up believing that ghouls were only Halloween illusion.

Actually the affection with which I now regard my childhood surprises me. Twenty years ago, all I could see were its shortcomings, my own embarrassing naiveté, the racial bigotry, the narrow perspective, the time we wasted practicing cheerleader routines or "dragging" the Dairyette on New Boston Road when we could have been, well, reading Dostoevski.

At forty, perhaps I've unconsciously done some editing of the memories and come to treasure a time and a place that allowed such gradual maturing. As one friend who shared that childhood said recently, "In that small pond, we grew up believing everything was within our reach. We edited the school paper, played the piano, performed in the senior play, led cheers for football heroes whom we also tutored in English grammar, memorized about half of the King James Bible, sang tenor in the church choir until the boys' voices changed, wrote skits for Y-Teens, gave patriotic speeches to the Rotary Club and won essay contests sponsored by the D.A.R. The self-confidence, even if it was unwarranted, carried us a long way." Indeed, a taste for truffles and brie could be acquired in due season.

Sixties activist Abbie Hoffman was recently quoted as saying, "Frankly, I don't trust anyone under thirty." While I was never really a part of Hoffman's world, I sympathize. I came of age in the South (East Texas is not the West) somewhere between the "hoods" and the "hippies." We discarded bobby socks in college but not bras. Soap operas in my day were only important to retired people like my aunt Lois, who was downright abusive to anyone who called during "As the World Turns." My generation does not do its work to blaring rock music, nor do we use the word "really" as an affirmation. We are a little suspicious of those who do. My drug-free rebellious years were accompanied by idealistic folk singers. My sons refer to this music as Mother's "peace-not-war-nut" music. Well, what do kids sing at camp or on school bus trips if they don't know "Blowin' in the Wind"? I rather like the fact that the heartthrobs of my teenage years are occasionally evoked by a grocery store rendition of an old Johnny Mathis or Frank Sinatra tune. I can hum my own nostalgia. How will they hum a heavy metal composition?

Mine is perhaps the last generation of women for whom Anglo-Saxon four-letter words retain some shock value and therefore offer some real therapeutic catharsis. It troubles me to hear the kid in the line at Baskin-Robbins yell "F———" just because they've run out of jamoca almond fudge. What does he have left to yell when he runs out of gas in August on Central Expressway during rush hour?

In my forties, I suppose I'll have to work at bridging these gaps or risk being called an old f——— (in public) before my time.

While I don't approach this new decade with debilitat-

ing regrets, the list of "things left undone which we ought
to have done" by now seems endless. I've never been to
San Francisco. I meant to be fluent in French at thirty. I
can't play tennis. I intended to grow my hair long like
Gloria Steinem's just once and wear it in a long Indian
braid down my back. It was too curly when that was fash-
ionable, and now that three pregnancies have straight-
ened it sufficiently, my face seems to require a little curly
diversion. Book I of Bach's *Well-Tempered Clavier* is still
not mastered, and two books on the Middle East which
I've never finished reading glare at me from my bedside
table. I grew up with a father who sang "Oh, What a
Beautiful Mornin' " while he shaved and who always whis-
tled or hummed as he came in from a hard day. I meant to
have a singing family too. Oh, not the Trapps on tour—just
a tune or two to break the monotony of long car trips and
some serious harmony at Christmas. I'm an alto. I need
somebody to sing the melody.

I'm sure I was supposed to have a daughter by now. It's
hard to turn forty and accept the fact that this is it. A letter
dated June 15, 1904, from Clarksville, Texas, was written
to my grandmother on her birthday by her father. I saved
it and thought someday it would decorate my own daughter's room. It now hangs as a joke in the hallway between
my sons' bedrooms. It says:

Dear Daughter.

I always recall with a great deal of pleasure the day
the first girl came into our family. She was then a well-
spring of pleasure, a messenger of peace and love and
through all the years since, she has been a continued
source of joy and comfort. I can wish no greater boon

than that her children may grow up to bless her life as she has ours.

> This leaves us all well.
> Yours affectionately,
>
> A. P. Corley

I know from my friends who have daughters that girls are not guaranteed "wellsprings of pleasure." They write letters from camp that say, "Dear Mom, Don't puke. I have bleached my hair. One side looks okay, but the other side is greenish." They tend to be a source of "joy and comfort" only to their fathers. One shopping expedition with a thirteen-year-old girl would probably destroy my fantasies entirely. It's just that it gets lonely around here, in an all-male household, the wisdom of my experience is always suspect. It's girl stuff. They haven't the foggiest notion why I would treasure William's homemade valentine that says, somewhat elliptically,

Der Mom,
Rozs are red.
Vlts.

> I love you,
> William:

However, the richness of the past twenty years easily eclipses the regrets. I've had some irresistible and rewarding detours. The timing of the births of our children, which we certainly never planned, seems in retrospect to have been good. We predate the now avant-garde notion that having a baby and raising it is, after all, worthwhile. The fact is, no one was debating career versus motherhood when I had my first two babies, and by the time the third one came along I was old enough to appreciate the pleasures of limited ambition. A friend who published a best-selling first novel at forty said that she was frequently asked by younger female interviewers if she didn't regret all those years spent tending children when she could have been writing fiction. "Where do you think this novel came from?" she patiently replied.

I don't envy the forty-year-old career women who are writing rhapsodic essays on babies born just in the nick of time. Many of them will have to balance toddlers, dependent elderly parents and their own menopause simultaneously. I like the fact that I can still fly kites and ride a bicycle to the neighborhood pool with my boys. They sometimes insist that I ride a block behind because they are ashamed of my ancient bicycle, but at least it's the bike that embarrasses them, not me. Their dad, at forty-two, skis, fishes, hunts and plays sports with them. Almost every evening, against my pleading, he and the boys stage a "best two falls out of three" tag team match on the floor of our bedroom. I don't know how much longer John will be able to become the lurching old camel who carries long-legged William to bed on his back, or how much longer I'll be able to scale his bunk bed to read stories by flashlight in the cozy tent he's created, but I know that there are less satisfying ways to develop muscle spasm. I'm glad we started all of this in our twenties.

A well-meaning mother asked me not long ago if I had read a child-rearing tome called *Children as Wet Cement*. I haven't. The older my children get, the more I espouse genetic theories of child development. *I* am the wet cement. In addition to the stretch marks they brought initially, my boys as toddlers also curved my spine slightly as I balanced them on my right hip. They have worn down the grass in the front yard, my weight, my nutritional scruples and my lofty expectations. While I once may have harbored some hopes that they might win Nobel prizes, now I will be perfectly satisfied if they remember to write thank you notes. Grateful hearts can weather almost anything. My sons have elicited an unselfishness that I didn't know I had. They have demanded prayers before bedtime which inadvertently slowed us down and restored our faith. We have looked into feverish little faces with knitted brows and doled out wisdom and reassurance that sometimes banished our own middle-aged insomnia. They have expanded my memory for details to extraordinary proportions. Each fall, in addition to my own calendar, I memorize baroque schedules of music lessons, library days, soccer and football practices, car pools and, when I forget, Jack with his unforgiving elephant memory says, "Oh, now, Mom, you're getting just like Mrs. Sims."

"Mrs. Sims?"

"You know, James's mother who forgot the Cokes for our soccer game in the fourth grade."

The clutter of suburban detail perhaps explains why my male writer friends can ponder global problems of national defense and immigration while I'm lying awake nights trying to figure out a way to make Jack think being an acolyte at church was his idea. That's okay. The actuarial tables say that I'll outlive my male friends and I will have had ten years of bizarre, intimate life experience they never knew.

These have been good years. I champion the pleasures and perils of being at home with children in their early years, but I also acknowledge that having had a part-time, flexible career for the past decade makes this crossing into forty easier for me. While there are days when I think I can barely live with my children, I know that shortly I must live without them. The rock music reverberating from two separate bedrooms will suddenly cease. My typewriter, however, can hum right along for the next thirty or forty years. The writing and the paychecks have given me security and self-confidence apart from my role as mother. My boys are spared the burden of being my entire life's work. Books and magazine stories can be completed; children never are.

By all statistics, however, the real achievement of my past twenty years is my marriage. By some Providence, the history course grader who dated my lovely blond college roommate became the handsome wedding usher who seated me and whispered, "Do you need a ride to the reception?" The rest is history—nineteen years of it. We recently heard a marriage counselor at our church say that holding a marriage together takes dogged resolution. We've never felt doggedly resolute, but we've often joked that the reason we've made it together thus far is because we don't believe in "growth." Everyone we know who speaks of having "grown" or who has learned to "share" has also divorced. We are wary of trendy marriage vows that promise, "I will love you with confrontation." The world confronts us enough. The best marriages we know are comfortable, consoling retreats—places where we don't compete or write contracts.

Sharing the same interests is perhaps less important than we thought. About four years after John and I married, a woman confided to me that she feared ever completing the remodeling of her house. "It's the only thing that Joe and I have in common anymore," she admitted. That struck me as so very sad that I told John about it at dinner. Her lament became a touchstone validating the closeness of our own relationship. It still pops up from time to time. John loathes being read to. Well, he'll dutifully listen to William's first-grade primers, but he shrinks from a well-crafted paragraph by V. S. Pritchett that I want him to hear. Exasperated one evening, I yelled, "We used to read the same books. You were the literary ace in college. Now if the CIA doesn't figure in the story you won't read it." He put his Ludlum down and said, "Shall we add a wing or build a pool?"

He fly-fishes and plays tennis. I read literary tomes and play the piano. He's compulsive and loves lists. I work on whim and inspiration and never in a straight line. There are mysterious compatible rhythms in it all somewhere. We are very lucky.

There is perhaps something to be said for marrying someone of equal intelligence, but as the years go by I've come to appreciate the compatibility of equal incompetence. John allows William to listen to the end of "Star Wars" on the car radio in the driveway and has a dead battery on Monday morning. I misread the airline tickets and we have to do the O. J. Simpson routine to make it to the last terminal. We both steadfastly pay the most money for the least possible service. Is there an ad in the Yellow Pages that says, "If you didn't sell it to the Mackintoshes, you didn't get the best price!"? We fly by the seat of our pants most of the time, trying to juggle three boys, a needy old house, a dog in heat and the car that needs jump starting. Who has the energy for recrimination or confrontation?

I think it also helps to have similar physical infirmities. Sinusitis afflicts us both, and we're certain that no one else could put up with us at this point. A marriage with Kleenex snowfall on only one side of the bed would no doubt require some dogged resolution.

If someone had put a sign in my yard on my birthday proclaiming PRUDENCE IS FORTY, I think I might have penciled across the bottom, "Maybe she always was." I bid my thirties and girlhood (it lasts longer in Texas) farewell and greet the new decade with optimism, lucky in love and work and good friends. I won't throw out my eyelash curler, but I won't expect to win the rock station disc jockey's "Pretty Young Thing" contest in which Drew entered me last week. The contest prize—a six-pack of Pepsi and a dozen red roses from the Rose Stop—would be nice, but I think it's wisdom we're after now.

> Some work of noble note, may yet be done. . . .
> 'Tis not too late to seek a newer world. . . .
> Though much is taken, much abides; and though
> We are not now that strength which in old days
> Moved earth and heaven; that which we are, we are—
> One equal temper of heroic hearts,
> Made weak by time and fate, but strong in will
> To strive, to seek, to find, and not to yield.

May I recite that aloud? We even memorized Tennyson back in my day.